WHAT THEY SAY ABOUT

"This is *good stuff!* If any job seekers really follow this 30-day plan, they should have success long before then!"

—**Robert O. Snelling, Sr., chairman of the board, Snelling and Snelling, Inc., the world's largest professional employment service**

"This is the first employment book I've seen that breaks away from all the old clichés of resume writing and networking and applies some new techniques from modern marketing and journalism to help determined people find jobs in the shortest possible time."

—**Ron Hoff, former creative director of Ogilvy & Mather, Inc., and Foote, Cone & Belding, and author of *I Can See You Naked***

"I have interviewed many job candidates over the years and I wish all of them had read *30 Days to a Good Job* before coming to see me. They could have targeted their resumes and interviews to my organization's needs much more directly and stood a much better chance of getting the position. It is indeed a great book for our current time."

—**Ed Stone, former vice-president of marketing for Opryland USA (Opryland Theme Park, Grand Ole Opry, and TNN–The Nashville Network), president, Ed Stone & Associates**

"*30 Days to a Good Job* has the missing ingredient! A day-by-day plan for making your job hunt pay off!"

—**Joyce Lain Kennedy, nationally syndicated careers columnist (*Los Angeles Times* Syndicate)**

"30 Days to a Good Job looks like a winner. A timely, savvy briefing for the job hunter. It offers new ways to reach the right employers and good advice on what to do next. It should be the job hunter's first investment."

—Neil Morgan, associate editor, *San Diego Union-Tribune*

"30 Days to a Good Job is brimming with intelligent insights and rock-solid suggestions. This book marches you along smartly toward a successful conclusion of your search for a new job."

—Richard Janssen, former senior editor, *Business Week*

"Should provide a very useful and thorough guide to finding civilian jobs for military people facing the additional challenge of translating military experience and training into equivalent civilian job qualifications."

—Gene Conner, Rear Admiral, U.S. Navy (RET.)

30 DAYS TO A GOOD JOB

The Systematic Job-hunting Program That Will Help You Find Profitable Employment in One Month or Less

HAL GIESEKING & PAUL PLAWIN

A FIRESIDE BOOK • PUBLISHED BY SIMON & SCHUSTER

New York   London   Toronto   Sydney   Tokyo   Singapore

FIRESIDE
Rockefeller Center
1230 Avenue of the Americas
New York, New York 10020

DESIGNED BY BARBARA MARKS
Manufactured in the United States of
America

10 9 8 7 6 5 4 3 2 1

Library of Congress Cataloging-in-Publication Data
Gieseking, Hal.
    30 days to a good job : the systematic job-
hunting program that will help you find profitable
employment in one month or less / Hal
Gieseking & Paul Plawin.
        p.   cm.
    "A Fireside book"—CIP t.p.
    Rev. ed. of: Get a good job in 30 days.
    1. Job hunting—Handbooks, manuals, etc.
I. Plawin, Paul, date.   II. Gieseking, Hal. Get a
good job in 30 days.   III. Title.   IV. Title: Thirty
days to a good job.
HF5382.7.G54   1994
650.14—dc20   93-44994
                                                              CIP

ISBN: 0-671-88127-2

Previously published under the title *Get a
Good Job in 30 Days*

Contents

Foreword

Congratulations!

By starting this program you are making a commitment to devote all of your energy and talents for a 30-day period to getting a job.

Fortunately for you, most other job seekers are unwilling or unable to make this commitment. They pursue their search in an episodic way, governed by alternating moods of elation and despondency. They may send out hundreds of cover letters and resumes aimed at vague, shadowy targets they know little or nothing about. Then they complain (both predictably and accurately), "Nothing works!"

But you are about to approach the job market in a systematic, dedicated way—by identifying your job targets with care, learning all you can about them, and pursuing them relentlessly using old and new techniques that separate you from your competition.

Every day of the search, we'd like you to keep in mind three thoughts that are at the core of almost every successful job search today.

1. The *more* contacts you make with individuals who have the authority to hire you, the *faster* you will find employment.
2. People who most successfully communicate how their skills, education, and past work experiences can *add value* to an organization will far outdistance other job applicants.
3. All other factors being equal, "hiring authorities" choose those people they *like* (for example, those they think will fit in best with the company, with co-workers and supervisors, with clients and customers, and with the industry).

During this 30-day program you can become a much more responsive person by approaching each day and even each rejection as a learning experience. You will also learn to fine-tune your job search by employing proven job-getting techniques and creative new ideas.

In short, you will become the type of enthusiastic, problem-solving individual most organizations *want* to hire today to help them survive and prosper in an increasingly complex local, national, and international marketplace. Remember Dale Carnegie's quick tip on building rapport: "You can make more friends in two months by becoming interested in other people than you can in two years by trying to get other people interested in you."

We wish you much good fortune in your job search. We will do everything we can in the following pages to help you hear these words as quickly (and as often) as possible: "We want you to come to work for us."

—HAL GIESEKING and PAUL PLAWIN

Part I

Getting Ready

It's no shame to be poor. But it's no great honor either.

—FIDDLER ON THE ROOF

Today's Turbulent Job Market

Over the years, search and rescue teams have noted a curious quirk common among hunters and hikers. When they lose their way in unknown territory, they start to *run* as fast as they can. This, unfortunately, is the worst thing to do, since in a few minutes they become exhausted, often fall and injure themselves, and/or seriously deplete their already limited body warmth and energy. Then their desperation increases to the point that they go to the other extreme—they find a place to huddle and do nothing.

In today's corporate America, when some people lose their jobs, they may exhibit similar behavior. First they "run" to any and all of their friends, asking for job leads. Then they throw together a disorganized resume and an indiscriminate cover letter and mail it to virtually every help-wanted ad remotely related to their interests and qualifications. And, of course, they call dozens of personnel offices. In the meantime, they may rush right past many "hidden" job opportunities, never knowing they even existed. After several days or weeks, they may discover that their energy and resources are depleted, and they sink into helpless despondency on the living room couch. At that point, their job search effectively ends.

We believe there's a much better, more effective way to find a good job in America today and to cut days or even weeks off your search. We have developed a 30-day job-getting program that applies time management and structure to tried and true techniques that have helped millions of people find good jobs. We also provide a continuous flow of new ideas to give you the creative edge on your competitors. This program provides day-by-day guidance to help you reach the maximum number of people who can put you on the payroll in the shortest possible time. It begins by helping you take a realistic look at yourself and at the job market today. If you're a new job hunter in the dense woods of unemployment, it helps to know the territory.

The American job market is chaotic and frequently illogical. Your deepest suspicions are correct. Jobs often *do not* go to the most qualified, the most experienced, or the hardest workers. Organizations may hire people they know or those who propitiously appear at the time of the opening. But they may also hire people who "package" themselves most effectively relative to the needs of the company.

Today the ideal job hunter would have a combination of attributes—the organizational skills and creativity of Ben Franklin, the good-humored adaptability of Erma Bombeck, the marketing skills of David Ogilvy, the handicapping smarts of a Las Vegas bookmaker—all with the stamina and will to win of Attila the Hun.

Even the superperson resulting from such a genetic breakthrough could still run headlong into the buzz saw of words heard by so many laid-off mid-level executives who have recently hit the streets:

"Overqualified."

"Not hiring."

"Try again in six months."

That's because the Great American Job Machine "ain't what she used to be."

In the past 13 years Fortune 500 corporations have laid off

enough people to populate Minneapolis and Phoenix (some 4.4 million workers). More managers and white-collar workers have picked up unemployment checks in the last five years than at any other time in American history. Even when business conditions improve, many large and small companies alike are postponing new hires. Instead they are authorizing more overtime by already overworked employees, or using part-time, temp, or contract workers to handle the new business.

Economists tell us that among the reasons for these seismic employment changes are corporate concerns about staying competitive in the new global marketplace and advanced technology that often replaces people with computers. Another factor is the growth of the hidden costs of hiring a new employee, such as retirement and health benefits. Whatever the reasons, the word "downsizing" has become a frequently heard and wildly unpopular addition to our language.

If you're a regular reader of the business pages, you probably can recite each and every one of the above reasons right along with us. If you've recently been part of a "downsizing," you *are* the news. You already know the sadness, bitterness, and confusion that can sweep over everyone who is suddenly unemployed. But, most of all, you keep asking yourself one question:

What do I do now?

In this book we provide an answer to that question.

Unlike most writers of job-hunting books, we are not current or former human resources directors, personnel directors, or headhunters. Our background is on the other side of the desk. We are writing colleagues who have spent a number of years looking for (and finding) jobs in boom times and bad. We have found good positions in journalism, marketing, advertising, and public relations and have handled special assignments for companies that include Meredith Corporation, Ogilvy & Mather, Grey Advertising, CBS, Kiplinger Washington Editors, Reader's Digest, VISA, and American Express. The average period of unemployment for both of us combined has been less than 20 days.

You probably remember the story of why the hare outran the fox. The fox was running for its dinner. The hare was running for its *life.* This book is written entirely from the job hunter's point of view by reasonably successful hares, for people who *have* to find jobs.

We have always been able to get jobs quickly—and not be cause we were the brightest or the best-qualified applicants. It's just that we had independently developed similar job-hunting systems that included:

Personal goal setting. What type of job and lifestyle did we want and where did we want to live?

Research. How did others in our industry and occupational specialties find jobs and what were the needs and problems of companies in the industry?

Packaging. How could we identify and best communicate those facts about our past work experiences that were most likely to meet the needs of the organizations we wanted to work for?

Developing a creative edge: We knew that every good job attracts highly competent competitors. We learned that it's important to do something that attracts favorable attention and distinguishes you from others who have alarmingly similar (or even better) credentials. (To give ourselves that creative edge, we applied a number of underused tools from journalism and from advertising and marketing that we will share with you in this program.)

Creating a structure: We followed the same daily work routine throughout the search as we would in a regular job. No trips to the beach. No afternoon movies. Just a firm 9 A.M. to 5 P.M. routine.

Not giving up: We kept going in the face of limited or no response.

WE BEGAN THIS book with several goals in mind. We wanted to:

- Identify the techniques used by those individuals who have been successful in finding good jobs in a few days or weeks.
- Create a matrix of what works in today's employment market.
- Keep the book short. People who are out of work don't need a lengthy tome on the intricacies of the employment world. They simply want to know what works—how they can get a job in the shortest possible time. Unemployment is too expensive.

What Works?

Dozens of books and articles have been written in recent years about job hunting. Many are really excellent, providing ideas for "killer resumes," how to write great cover letters, how to survive "stress" interviews, etc. We have reviewed most of them and condensed their best ideas in this book, creating a job-hunter's digest of tips and techniques. We have supplemented this research by interviewing many executives of employment and outplacement firms, CEOs, directors of human resources, and "hiring authorities" (bosses, supervisors, and department heads with the power to put people on the payroll overnight).

While these experts may disagree among themselves about resume formats and interview techniques, there is virtual unanimity on certain key points:

Most jobs today are obtained through *networking* (phone, mail, or personal contact with people who can hire you, give you job leads and information about companies, or refer you to others who can provide this kind of help). No reputable job authority disagrees with this assessment. The accompanying chart demonstrates the power of frequent contacts and how dramatically it can shorten the length of your job search.

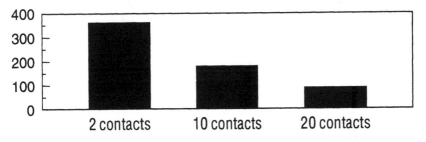

The POWER of Frequent Contacts
Length of Job Search in Number of Days

From a survey by Goodrich & Sherwood Co.

In our program you will make 70 contacts weekly.

Most experts estimate that networking accounts for between 60 and 90 percent of all new employment. In a few industries networking is the only way to get a job. The three other most effective ways to find jobs (but they trail far behind networking) are *employment agencies, recruitment advertising,* and *direct mail* to companies.

Between 70 and 80 percent of all jobs are never advertised anywhere (another average of experts' estimates). This is another way of saying these are jobs that are usually filled by networking. This so-called "hidden job market" includes the thousands of jobs that open up each day because of natural transition as people retire, quit, move to another city, get fired, pass away, go back to school, or switch careers. For days or even months before these openings are posted by the personnel department or advertised, they can languish in the "hidden" job market as supervisors or department heads look for someone they know or wait for corporate authorization to hire a replacement. Anyone who by search, chance, or (primarily) networking becomes aware of these openings has a golden opportunity to apply—with virtually no competition. Those who wait for the help-wanted ads can get caught in a riptide of other applicants.

Most new jobs are generated by small companies (100 employees or less), and these companies are often located in small communities. A recent survey by Dun & Bradstreet estimated that about 80 percent of all new jobs in 1993 were generated by companies with fewer than 100 employees. Joseph W. Duncan, corporate economist for D&B, said: "In contrast, the nation's largest firms expect a net decline of employment [in 1993]."

No company today wants to hire more employees. Employees are expensive—in salary, space required, and benefits. Companies hire only people who offer *more value* to the organization than what they will cost. If you can demonstrate your ability to help solve problems, increase profits or efficiency, or reduce costs, chances are you'll go directly to the head of the line.

When companies hire new employees, they usually spend about *90 percent of their search time screening applicants* and only about 10 percent deciding which of the remaining five or ten survivors to hire. Even tiny mistakes (such as misspellings in your correspondence and resumes) can rule you out when screeners are looking for every possible reason to narrow the pile of qualified applicants.

People can usually shorten their job search if they possess certain *transferable skills* that can be used in a number of different industries. For example, if you were an engineer with a CAD computer background, you could adapt those skills to a wide variety of industries. If, however, you decided a job search was just the time to renew yourself as a landscape gardener, you probably would have a very long job search. Some people do make such great career leaps successfully, but the odds are against them. Finding a job quickly means always keeping the odds on your side.

How can you be sure to keep the odds in your favor in this professional jungle? Of course, you need to send out great resumes and cover letters. You must also be able to shine through multiple interviews. In this program we'll review these basics with you. *But keep in mind that all these skills have now become just the price of admission to the top cut in today's job market.*

Let's better your odds by giving your job search a daily structure. Remember how efficient you were in your previous position? That's because you probably operated within a 9 A.M. to 5 P.M. time frame, with specific assignments to perform before noon and in the afternoon. This program will require the same kind of structure, providing you with special assignments each day. These assignments are heavily weighted toward the three major areas of job-finding probability: *networking* (which involves about 60 percent of your time), followed by *work with employment agencies and headhunters*, and *research*, which helps you to develop creative responses to job prospects and recruitment ads.

WE STRONGLY RECOMMEND that you operate your job search like a business. We'll give it the working title of You, Inc. You will be asked to set up a budget, prepare all your basic working tools (from stationery and resumes to business cards and filing systems), and delegate a number of the research assignments in this program either to willing members of your family or to part-time help.

A survey by the human resources firm of Goodrich & Sherwood showed that a job hunter who saw only two companies a week could expect to look for work for at least a year. But job hunters who contacted 10 prospective employers a week found work within six months. During this program you will be asked to contact at least 70 hiring authorities each week. That may sound like a discouragingly high number, but we consider every phone call, letter, or meeting you have with someone a contact. In fact, if you use a computer and some of the new contact telephone software, you should be able to increase that to almost 100 contacts a week. (See Chapter Seven on using research.) Some professional sales people make 25 to 100 contacts *a day*.

It's not going to be easy, but you probably didn't think it would be. But we're going to work with you every step of the way to create a job-getting system that grows more powerful every day.

Before You Begin . . .

Here are the questions most frequently asked about the 30-Days to a Good Job program.

Q. *I just lost my job. Should I start right into this 30-day program?*

A. No, we suggest you take a few days to consider your next steps. You should acknowledge any feelings of bitterness or sadness you feel about the job loss. These are perfectly natural emotions. Some psychologists suggest you write down your feelings. Judy Hamilton, client manager of the outplacement firm of Schoenberg Associates in Indianapolis, tells of one recently fired client who went to a garage sale and bought a set of old dishes. Then she went home to her garage and smashed every dish against the wall!

Be sure to express these emotions so you can get them out of the way and make a fresh start. However, don't go on vacation. Job counselors say this disrupts your established work ethic. It also could use up funds you will need for a quick, successful job hunt.

You can also be much more effective during the 30-day program if you make basic preparations at least one or two weeks before you begin: Print stationery and resumes, set up You, Inc., and prepare your Life Experience and Job Prospect cards and set up your Contact Notebook, as explained in the chapters that follow.

Q. *Isn't it unrealistic today to expect to find a job in 30 days?*

A. We don't think so. It's true that some people have been looking for work for two years or more. But we also know of others who have found work within several days of losing their previous jobs.

According to the U.S. Bureau of Labor Statistics, in 1992 the median hunting time for all workers before they found a position was 8.8 weeks. This median was lengthened by those who dropped in and out of the job market, or who spent weeks approaching companies that didn't need people with their skills, or who did not clearly communicate what they could offer.

If you research and target the companies most likely to need someone with your background, and if you contact enough people within those companies with a careful presentation of what you can do, you can cut days, weeks, even months off your job-search time.

Q. *What is the most common mistake among job hunters?*

A. They give up on an organization too quickly. Perhaps they send a letter and resume to the human resources department of a large company. Maybe they get no response or a form letter of rejection. They then say, "Chrysler isn't hiring," or, "Apple Computers turned me down."

That's absurd! One individual at that company rejected their application. But there are hundreds—sometimes thousands—of others at that same company who have the authority and funds to hire people. These include department heads, supervisors, foremen, and various company officers. We call them *hiring authorities*.

Even small companies may have a number of people who can hire you, from the boss to the marketing director to the head of the shipping department.

Your search has barely begun when you contact one or two

people in a company. If you use each contact (and rejection) as a means to gather additional names of other company executives and more information about how that company operates, you're better prepared when you call the next person in line.

Most companies are also moving parades. The person who rejected your application last week could be looking for a new job this week! Companies' needs change day by day. As in roulette, if you've played only one chip, you're barely in the game.

Shortly after Hal Gieseking graduated from college, his mother gave him a copy of a book, *Confessions of an Advertising Man,* by David Ogilvy. He said after reading the book, "I felt I was in the presence of an eccentric genius, and his words confirmed my desire to go into advertising." When he came to New York City more than a decade later, he met with Clifford Field, who was then creative director of Ogilvy & Mather, Inc. Field was not impressed by the ad portfolio Gieseking presented and turned him down. Several weeks later he applied to the agency's personnel director and received a quick response: "O&M is not hiring." Two weeks later he saw the name of Ron Hoff, one of several dozen of the agency's creative supervisors, in a trade magazine. He wrote to him. After Hoff interviewed Gieseking and reviewed the same ad portfolio that Field had previously seen, he hired the writer within two days. Gieseking then worked eight years at that agency.

Q. *I have been looking for work now for several months and getting little or no feedback from companies. Even when I get an interview, the companies don't call me back. What's happening?*

A. You should review your entire application procedure, from cover letter to the answers you give in interviews. The suggestions in this program should help.

You also should check two other possible roadblocks that you may not have been aware of—your credit rating and your references.

In the final hiring stages, most employers may check both very carefully. If you have problems with your credit rating (a personal bankruptcy or a series of unpaid credit card accounts), this could raise a red flag. The irony is that some of the notations could be there by mistake.

To check your current record with a major credit-rating firm, send your written request to TRW, P. O. Box 2350, Chatsworth, CA 91313-2350. Print your name, spouse's first name, address, year of birth, and social security number on a sheet of paper—along with other addresses you may have had in the past five years. Enclose a photocopy of your current driver's license or a bill from a major creditor as proof of your current address. You are entitled to one free credit check each year. If you see any statement that is incorrect, contact TRW immediately.

Another possible hidden roadblock is the quality of your references. Most companies today are checking references carefully. Some references, particularly former supervisors at your previous jobs, are very concerned about giving you a bad reference for fear of being sued. They may give a neutral endorsement, acknowledging that you worked at a certain job for a period of time, but saying little else. Such endorsements are the equivalent of being damned by faint praise. Even some people you felt would give you enthusiastic references could disappoint you. To be sure that poor references aren't hindering your job search, ask a friend to write a letter to your references asking them to provide a candid appraisal of you. You might be pleasantly (or unpleasantly) surprised by what they say. In any case, you should know. Then you can cite your most enthusiastic supporters as references, and quietly drop the others.

For a fee, Taylor Review will discretely check out your references. For more information, call 800-782-5720.

Q. *Why do you suggest sending a cover letter and resume to the CEO of every job prospect? Aren't these people too busy to respond?*

A. Many job hunters feel that way, so they apply further down the corporate ladder. Yet at smaller companies (where most of the hiring action is today), the president is frequently the one who makes hiring and firing decisions.

Even with larger companies, there are advantages to starting at the top. Thomas Christensen, Executive Vice President of Citizens Federal Bank in Fort Lauderdale, Florida, told us: "Most CEOs get few resumes because many job hunters wouldn't think of sending their resume to them. CEOs often don't know the specific hiring needs of their department heads. But if they see a resume that looks good, they will bounce it down to the appropriate department head—or even to all department heads. These people will consider the resume carefully *because* it came from the CEO."

Q. *What time management techniques do you recommend?*

A. There are several ways to make effective use of your time.

1. Set daily short-term goals for yourself. Some of your "assignments" will already be waiting for you as you follow our program. But you may want to add other projects of your own. At the end of each day, make a note of which projects or contacts you were unable to complete, and carry them over to the next day.

2. Maintain a good filing system and a clean work space. This allows you to concentrate on the project at hand without spending hours sifting through piles in search of a lost letter.

3. Delegate. Get research help. You must have complete, accurate, up-to-date information on companies and industries. We realize that many job hunters are watching every penny, but there is no reason why a good assistant couldn't gather this under your guidance, and most will work for modest fees. For example, in preparing this manuscript the authors received expert secretarial assistance for $6 to $8 an hour. The best use of your time is making direct contact with hiring authorities.

Work with a secretarial service, use a computer, or get correspondence help from a spouse or friend. Create a series of several basic letters. Then use the boilerplate approach to customize them.

Example: Look through your Life Experience Cards (these are explained in Chapter Four). Number the resume bullets at the bottom of each card. Then let's say you are writing to a manufacturing concern that needs someone with TQM (total quality management) experience. You have just such experience, but it's not mentioned in either your cover letter or resume. On the standard form letter, write some notes in red to your secretarial help—"Add 1," "Add 5," "Add 7"—with arrows showing where you want this information to go.

Your secretarial help can then pick up this information and

add it to the letter. It's even much simpler if you have a computer. These alternate paragraphs can be stored under different file names and dropped into the basic letter wherever you designate.

4. Make every action count at least twice. *Example:* You call someone within one of your targeted companies but are repeatedly blocked by his or her secretary. Ask that person for the name of other people within that company that you should call. Or ask for the company's annual report. Before Thomas Edison invented the electric light bulb, he was asked if he was discouraged by his 5,000 earlier experiments that had failed to create light. Edison was surprised by the question, as he saw the experiments not as failures but as methods of collecting information. He then knew something no other inventor did—5,000 ways *not* to create electric light.

Q. *What if I don't find a job in 30 days?*

A. We strongly recommend that you take a weekend to relax. Then start the program all over again. During the first month you will have contacted dozens of hiring authorities and stirred embers in organizations throughout your industry. Any one of those activities could lead to a job within the next few days or weeks.

You will have become a much more savvy job hunter than you were just 30 days earlier. You will have learned (or relearned) some of the basic techniques that have gotten millions of people jobs through the years. You will have practiced new ideas and developed a creative edge, separating you from your competitors—all within a structured time-management program that helped you make more contacts than you may have ever thought possible.

You have managed your own new company, You, Inc., serving as CEO and sales manager, treasurer, and personnel director, learning valuable business lessons that will increase your value to any future employer.

Keep in mind that there are many ways to make money other than a traditional job. You could work for temp agencies (which now also hire executives for part-time work). You could also work for a company on a contract basis for a predetermined period of time. Both temp and contract work are the fastest growing employment trends in America today.

You could even start your own business at home (where some 38 million Americans now work)! But, best of all, you will have learned the concept of added value. No one (except perhaps a relative) will hire you simply because you need a job. Employees are just too expensive today. Organizations will hire you only when you prove to them that the added value you bring exceeds the costs of having you on board.

Thinking like a Winner

Human beings can alter their lives by altering their attitudes.

—WILLIAM JAMES

One of the most important steps you can take before beginning your job search is to take a serious look at yourself. People with "an attitude" may search for work twice as long as others because no one wants to hire them.

Were you laid off recently? Do you feel bitter? If you're like many other recently laid-off Americans, you may be seething with resentment. After all, the company had no right to fire you. You were doing a good job. You put your heart and soul into that company, and they threw you out the door like a broken piece of machinery. It's not *fair!*

Of course, it's not fair. But as M. Scott Peck's best-seller *The Road Less Traveled* begins, "Life is difficult." Peck wisely points out that once we truly understand and accept that fact—that life *is* difficult—we stop expecting it to be "fair." And we get on with our lives.

Bitterness toward your former employer or a lack of self-esteem can directly affect your chances of finding a new job quickly. Companies won't hire people who rag on their former employers. And they quickly pass over job candidates who show no self-confidence in their own abilities.

Judi Dash, a former editor for a New Jersey newspaper, recounted her personal ordeal when she was fired in an article in the March 16, 1993, issue of *Family Circle* magazine. "Lacking motivation, I sat on my couch still dressed in my pajamas, drinking coffee late into each afternoon. Then I'd switch to my bed and watch television all night. I bathed sporadically and washed my hair only when it got too stringy to bear. After all, what was the point? There was nowhere I had to be, nowhere people would see me. My mind, when it could focus at all, raced back and forth between extremes: I would whisk out my resume and pound the pavement looking for a job. No, I would take six months and do nothing but play. No, I would go back to school. No, I would . . ."

You may even be blaming yourself for your recent dismissal. But, in the great majority of layoffs today, the employees have nothing to do with it. Perhaps they were laid off because some foreign company paying poverty wages could produce a cheaper widget. Or because the USSR, once the Great Satan, has become an indigent pussycat, and millions of dollars are now being trimmed from U.S. defense spending. Or because hundreds of thousands of American companies are now restructuring their businesses. They call it "downsizing" or "rightsizing," but what it really means is that many organizations are now working with the fewest number of employees possible to sustain their business. Instead of recalling laid-off workers or hiring new people as sales improve, these companies often bring in temp or contract workers to take up the slack. Regardless, you hope and send out dozens—sometimes hundreds—of letters and resumes but get little response. You answer every help-wanted ad you see. But no one writes or calls back. You live in Rejectionville, USA.

Life isn't fair. But do you know what happens when you give into these feelings of bitterness or disappointment?

Nothing.

You stop sending out letters and resumes. You stop making phone calls. And that practically *guarantees* you won't find a job.

Psychologists say you should acknowledge these feelings of bitterness by writing them down. You may have every right to feel unhappy. But remember that emotion is counterproductive for your future happiness. Many of us, when depressed, tend to go to an extreme and say, "I will never get a job." But psychologists also tell us you can—and should—learn to dispute such extreme thoughts. For a number of years you may have been productive and gainfully employed. Nothing has changed in *you*. Your resume lists your past accomplishments. The employer who will hire you will feel confident that you can repeat that success. You should read your own resume and give yourself the same credit employers do—the credit you deserve.

Something changed the minute you started this program. You made a conscious decision to try to do something to change your life. The best antidote for that "Woe is me" feeling is activity, and you are about to become *very active* for the next 30 days!

How Did Ben Do It?

Ben Franklin was a statesman, publisher, author, and printer. He was one of the prime movers behind the American Revolution. Oh, and in his spare time he also invented bifocal glasses, the lightning rod, and the Franklin stove. How did he find the time for all of this? He structured each of his days, lining up specific tasks to be performed each hour. Here is the text of Franklin's original daily calendar.

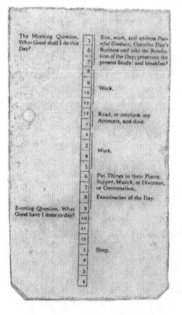

If you put structure in your day and perform each task to the best of your ability, you can move mountains. And *get a good job in 30 days!*

Part II

Mastering the Tricks of the Trade

I felt as if I were walking with destiny and that all my past life had been but a preparation for this hour and this trial. . . . I thought I knew a great deal about it all, and I was sure I should not fail. Therefore, although impatient for the morning, I slept soundly and had no need for cheering dreams. Facts are better than dreams.

—WINSTON CHURCHILL
THE SECOND WORLD WAR

Determining Your

Added Value

> - *Photocopy at least 100 Life Experience Cards from the end of this section.*
> - *Analyze the skills, education, and work experience you can bring to potential employers.*

"You already know more than you think you do," wrote Dr. Benjamin Spock. He was writing to nervous new parents, but the advice applies similarly to job seekers.

As a new job hunter, you may have much more to offer companies than you ever dreamed possible—including your education and all the skills and experiences you've gathered in your previous jobs and as a volunteer—when you attended trade shows, traveled, taught class, gave speeches, sold ideas and services, and engaged in many other activities that require "hidden" talents that you can and should consider when assessing your professional life.

If you know how to take inventory of these diverse items and then "package" those that most closely match the stated needs of a company looking for help, you are head and shoulders above other job candidates who simply send out "cookie cutter" resumes. You've given yourself the creative edge.

In short, don't rest on your laurels. *Sell them.* It's easier than you think.

Using the Life Experience Cards

On page 35 we have printed one 4″ × 6″ Life Experience Card, and completed one card on page 36 as a sample. We would like you to photocopy the blank-card page to create about 100 copies.

Your first project is to complete at least 50 of these cards, each with one of your experiences—or skills. Fill out a separate card for each one that comes to mind. Don't censor yourself.

Did you conduct a training class for your previous employer? Write it down.

Have you learned a foreign language? Write it down.

Did you ever attend a seminar on job productivity? Write it down.

Did you serve as a collector for a charitable fund-raising drive? Write it down.

Have you traveled overseas? Write it down.

You get the idea.

The first ones that come to mind will be the obvious ones. But keep digging. Ask family members and friends to remind you of some of your past activities. As you network with former co-workers, ask them about projects you worked on together. Look through company phone books for the names of former co-workers. This could help you recall projects you worked on. Examine past business papers and correspondence.

Now you have a stack of raw data about yourself.

After you've completed at least 50 of these cards, divide them into three piles:

- Projects I liked
- Project I didn't like
- Projects I was neutral about

Go through the "liked" pile. This will give you a quick reminder of some of your strengths and the types of projects you enjoy. The "didn't like" pile is just as valuable. It helps you recall and understand some of your possible weaknesses and jobs you might not enjoy. The "neutral" stack shows projects that you can at least tolerate.

Journalists often use index cards as the building blocks for an outline for an article or a book. You can use the same technique to organize data about yourself.

Now take one additional step. Analyze the results generated by any one of your experiences.

Let's say you helped set up a phone bank for volunteers collecting money for public television. Were there any new things you tried that made the evening more successful—for example, the number of phones you hooked up, or a system you developed to bring in local celebrities to increase the flow of phone calls and contributions? Record this information on the card in abbreviated form. Whatever your particular contribution to the event, turn it into a "bullet"—a short factual item that you could use in a resume or cover letter.

When you apply for a specific job, select just those bullets that most closely match the requirements of the position as it's stated in a help-wanted ad or in a job description. Think how much more powerful and targeted your cover letter and resume can be—light years ahead of competitors who simply write a standard cover letter and send out an all-purpose resume.

You will need one good all-purpose resume for blanket mailings or when you need to send out your qualifications instantly. But try creating a customized resume that matches your skills with specific job requirements when you know them. Write the job requirements on a large sheet of paper. Then put every card that looks like it might satisfy that requirement in a stack next to it. Your customized resume will virtually write itself as you select the most appropriate resume items.

Here are some other ways you can review your personal inventory of skills and aptitudes. Check with guidance and placement offices at local colleges. Many can give you vocational and aptitude tests at modest or no cost. Even if you are a seasoned executive and think you know yourself pretty well, you might be surprised to discover new skills you never thought you had.

You can also take an aptitude test by mail for less than $50, postpaid. For details, contact:

Chronical Guidance Publications
P.O. Box 1190
Moravia, NY 13118
315-497-0330

Psychological Assessment Resources
P.O. Box 998
Odessa, FL 33556
813-968-3003

Behaviorodyne
994 San Antonio Rd.,
Palo Alto, CA 94303
800-825-0673

We also recommend that you continue adding Life Experience Cards to your file even after you've landed your job. This file will continue to grow and may become even more useful as you build your career.

LIFE EXPERIENCE CARD

BRIEFLY DESCRIBE EXPERIENCE _____

WHERE? _____ WHEN? _____

NEW SKILLS OR KNOWLEDGE ACQUIRED _____

_____

_____

RESULTS: _____

_____

WRITE SHORT RESUME "BULLET":

●

Photocopy this page and cut to create copies of this card.

LIFE EXPERIENCE CARD

BRIEFLY DESCRIBE EXPERIENCE <u>Set up sales training classes for new life</u>

<u>insurance agents</u>

WHERE? <u>Norton Life Ins. Co.</u>   WHEN? <u>1989</u>

NEW SKILLS OR KNOWLEDGE ACQUIRED <u>Learned how to write an effective</u>

<u>training manual. New ability to research sales techniques using</u>

<u>computer databases</u>

RESULTS: <u>Classes "graduated" twenty agents; five became top</u>

<u>producers</u>

WRITE SHORT RESUME "BULLET":

• Created Sales Training Program for Norton Life Insurance

Company. Prepared sales manual for this course. Five of the

graduate agents sold $1,400,000 in insurance in just six months.

Describe the type of work or learning experience you gained from previous jobs, schools, seminars, travel, volunteer work, social activities, etc. These cards are invaluable in helping you create custom-made resumes and cover letters.

Describe any successful results because of your involvement—for example, an increase in sales, productivity, reduction of expenses, etc.

Name the organization where you gained this experience.

Now describe this experience in a way that demonstrates what added value you can bring to the fortunate company that hires you. Keep it short. Use action verbs and statistics. This is information that you can use to increase the power of each of your cover letters and resumes.

Establishing Your Goals

> • Set short-term goals each day of your job search and long-term goals for your life and career.

As working journalists, we have interviewed a number of people who have been extraordinarily successful, including Walter Cronkite, Jimmy Carter, Harold Geneen, Julia Child, William F. Buckley, Jr., James Michener, John Naisbitt, Jack Nicklaus, Buckminister Fuller, Herman Kahn, and others. While their views were wildly divergent in many areas, each person was goal driven.

Warren Bennis, Professor of Management at the University of Southern California and author of the book *Leaders,* says: "Many leaders are passionate dreamers. They have deeply felt convictions about what they want to achieve." Another thought expressed in self-achievement programs is that *goals are dreams with deadlines.*

Short-term goal setting can cut days or weeks off your job search. It allows you to concentrate on the types of work, the industry, and the location you prefer. Once you've identified your interests, you can then research only the most relevant information and avoid wasting time chasing will-o'-the-wisp jobs in far-flung places.

It's a good idea to write down your goals. Once you've put them in writing, they become potent "magnets" that you can use to direct and fine-tune your daily actions.

Where Do You Want to Work?

This is your single most important decision, because it can affect every aspect of your job search. Your decision can be based on many different factors. If you're single, unattached, and adventurous, you can choose virtually any part of the world for your search. If you're married with a family, your geographic options must involve family discussions and considerations, such as children in school and perhaps the income of your spouse if he or she is working. You also have to decide whether you will be comfortable emotionally leaving your support network of friends and relatives.

What Type of Job Do You Want? In Which Industry?

Conventional wisdom (which is conventional because it's frequently right) says you have a better chance of getting a job if you think you would like doing it. Your enthusiasm shows in your application and interview. By the same logic, your job goal should also be based on your aptitudes and past experience.

Even if you have transferable skills, we strongly recommend that you concentrate on choosing no more than two industries for your search. Otherwise you risk spreading your research too thin. Of course, there are always exceptions to the rule—people such as Lou Gerstner, who seems able to switch from top spots at American Express to Philip Morris and IBM without breaking stride. It also helps to be on the top of every headhunter's wish list!

You also have to decide on your salary requirements. You should probably be very flexible in order to remain competitive. You may have to take a lower salary in return for an opportunity of later advancement. Or you may have to accept less in order to stay within a certain geographic area.

WHAT WOULD YOU LIKE TO ACHIEVE IN THE NEXT FIVE YEARS?

Taking any job (even in today's fickle marketplace) could turn into a long commitment. When you receive a job offer, you have to evaluate if the position fits your career goals.

Remember that these goals are important but not etched in stone. You can make changes based on new information. *Flexibility is one of the key traits of people who find jobs in 30 days or less.*

Going to Work—
for You, Inc.

- *Create a daily workplace with phone, office tools, stationery, and files.*
- *Function like a business with the primary job of selling You.*

In a December 23, 1991, *Wall Street Journal* article, sales trainer Jack Falvey neatly summed up a new way to look at a job search in today's tight market.

"Out of work? Think again. You are really self-employed (with a deferred income). Your job is as senior sales representative and chief marketing officer. You are selling personal services—yours! And it is one of the most difficult jobs you will ever have."

Mr. Falvey is absolutely right—but we suggest that you carry this concept one step further: Set up your own job-getting business. As a working title, call it "You, Inc." because that's exactly what it is.

You accomplished a lot each day in your previous position. That is because you worked within a structure, either self-imposed or set by edicts and deadlines from department heads, CEOs, or colleagues.

You met deadlines, completed projects, and attended meetings because it was either part of your job or you were asked to handle it. Now that you're on your own, you still need that same kind of daily discipline and structure.

As CEO of your company, you are responsible for getting the most out of your principal employee—you. That means no two-hour lunches. The boss is watching. As marketing director of You, Inc., you must create and adhere to a marketing plan to ensure that you are targeting your time toward the most likely customers for your services. According to the marketing concept so many companies follow today, you are not selling what *you* want to sell. You are packaging and advertising your experiences to respond to what your job prospects want to buy. This 30-day job-hunting program provides you with a daily blueprint for your marketing activities, to which you can add your own creative ideas.

As treasurer, you must set up a monthly budget that includes specific amounts for your job-hunting activities (stationery, supplies, postage, travel, telephone, and secretarial services) as well as normal living expenses for you and your family. You can (and should) reduce your regular living expenses as much as possible, adjusting your lifestyle to skip filet mignon and season box seats.

But *don't* skimp on your job-marketing budget. Everything you send out should look first-rate—your stationery paper should be of a high rag content, typeset with your name and address; your resumes should be laser printed on high-quality bond (no "creative" colors, please); every exhibit of your past work should appear crisp and attractive. Remember that this "paper trail" is all that most prospective employers will see of you during the early days of your search. If anything looks shoddy, unprofessional, or dog-eared, employers may eliminate you from the pool of qualified applicants.

We also suggest you do something that sounds like sheer extravagance: *delegate*—the very thing that probably helped you accomplish so much in your previous job. But many job hunters, suddenly feeling poor, believe they have to do everything themselves to save money. Get at least one person to help you during your 30-day job search, and hire him or her if necessary. Of course, if you have a spouse, friend, or family member who will volunteer to handle secretarial and research assignments for you, count your blessings. If you don't have access to competent secretarial help, check the Yellow Pages under Secretarial Services. Another alternative is to place an ad in a neighborhood newspaper for a secretary (with computer or electric typewriter) who works at home. Interview applicants carefully, paying careful attention to the quality of their work. Ideally, you want to be able to store your basic correspondence and resumes on computer disk, with alternate paragraphs you can add to these basic formats when you apply to specific companies.

You can also benefit from hiring a research assistant. The ideal candidate would be a college junior or senior with a business major who wants part-time work and who is interested in finding work upon graduation in your chosen industry. Many of the daily assignments in our program call for a great deal of time spent in research. For the first few days, you will probably want to do the projects yourself. Later, if you can delegate research assignments to an assistant, you can spend much more of your day networking and making direct contact with the people who can hire you— that's where the action is.

If you are not completely comfortable with the quality of writing in your cover letters and other job correspondence, you may want to hire a professional writer. Check his or her credentials (and writing samples) carefully.

We realize that all of this represents extra expense, particularly at a time when you're hardly feeling expansive. But this kind of delegation is absolutely necessary to free up the hours necessary for you to concentrate on getting a job. Unemployment itself can be the greatest expense of all. For example, if you formerly earned $50,000 a year in salary and benefits, each day out of work is "costing" you about $192 in lost wages that can never be recovered. Spending the money to make a first-class presentation might just be the best investment you can make.

SETTING UP YOUR BUSINESS

Find a Quiet Place to Work

This can be anywhere from the kitchen table to the den in your home. If you have a friend who can provide you with desk space in an office, that's even better. You might even consider renting desk space in a nearby office for a month. The latter has the advantage of freeing you from home distractions.

Assemble, Buy, or Borrow Equipment

Telephone. The telephone is your primary job-hunting tool. You must have an answering service 24 hours a day. This can be either the voice-mail service provided by many local telephone companies or an answering machine. *You must not miss a single business call, day or night.* (Many out-of-town companies could call you during evening hours, especially from western states or overseas.) A call-waiting service that alerts you to another call coming in is another invaluable service.

Computer or Electric Typewriter. A computer with appropriate software, a modem, and a printer can be of tremendous help in shortening your job-search time (see Chapter Seven on using research). If you don't have or can't afford a computer, consider a barter arrangement with a neighbor or friend. Offer to help him or her paint a house or wallpaper a room after you have your job. You may even hire a college student who already has most of this equipment (many are incredible computer whizzes). At the very least, purchase an electronic typewriter with a new ribbon and clean keys (without filled-in a's, e's, or o's). You can now buy a new one with a correction function for $200 or less. Other pluses are a good copy machine and a fax. (Both of these services are also usually available at neighborhood business-service firms.)

Line up Outside Services

Make a list of addresses, available hours, and phone numbers for all outside services and people you may need during your job search, including:

Secretarial service or neighborhood secretary.
Copy and fax services (if you don't have your own). If you are registered with one of the local fax services, they will call you when a fax for you comes in.
Post office.
Nearest overnight delivery service.
Research assistant.

Set up Your Filing System

You'll need a file with at least two dividers to hold 4" × 6" index cards file that detail your job prospects and life experiences. (The latter are explained in Chapter Four, the former in Chapter Seven.)

Purchase large manila file folders to collect material on your specially targeted companies. Things like annual reports, ads, notes from interviews, etc., belong in these envelopes. You should also set up a file for each industry you want to enter or in which you have experience.

Prepare Your Paper Tools

When you have letterhead and envelopes printed with your name, address, phone number, and fax number, don't forget to use your title. You are not unemployed. You are just between engagements. You are an Engineer, a Marketing Consultant, a Computer Technician—whatever your chosen profession.

Business cards are also essential. Have some printed up (in two colors, if your budget will allow) with your name, title, address, phone number, and fax number.

Appointment Calendar. Keep this calendar by the telephone. Carry a pocket version with you at all times (with the same appointments marked). You want to be able to set up a job interview at any time. Keep your copy of *30 Days to a Good Job* next to your desk calendar. You will be referring to this book every day for the next month.

Contact Notebook. Many executives who successfully manage their time every day keep a large notebook right at the center of their desk. They write down every detail of every business call—who, when, what was discussed, the next steps to take—plus phone numbers and addresses. Trust us. If you hastily write down this information on odd or loose slips of paper, you are bound to lose important information and spend hours looking for it. Later in this chapter, we'll show you how to use this simple organizational technique most effectively.

Paper Supplies.

Stationery second sheets.
Large envelopes.
Folders that hold a resume and enclosures.
Overnight delivery envelopes.

You may want to set up an account with one of the overnight delivery services. Then you can drop your packages in their nearest collection box, using their shipping materials. You often will get a discount on their services by making this arrangement.

ASSEMBLE A JOB HUNTER'S BRIEFCASE

Carry this briefcase with you to every interview. It should include:

Five copies of your resume.
A small notebook.
An appointment calendar.
A city map/street directory (you do not want to get lost or be late for an interview).
Two ballpoint pens.
A page of business and personal references (give this out only when asked).
Any exhibits that you may want to present during the interview.
Your folder of research notes on that company—you can review it while you're waiting in the lobby.
Extra business cards.
Telephone credit card. In case one lengthy interview makes you late for a second interview, this card will allow you to call from the first company without getting a long stare from the secretary.

CONTACT NOTEBOOK

Tom Atkinson, an executive recruiter with Eric Kercheval & Associates in Minneapolis, offers this suggestion to job hunters: "Put a large looseleaf notebook in the center of your desk. Record every single phone call you make or receive. Record the names, titles, companies, and phone numbers of everyone you talk with—and any notes about follow-up actions. This can save you hours of time when you have to look up the name or number of someone you've talked with recently. It's also a much better system than recording all this information on miscellaneous note pads, backs of envelopes, etc.''

This is the Contact Notebook we referred to earlier, and it is an important business tool—so much so that we use it daily in our own work.

We've created a special Contact Notebook format for this program.

Obtain a standard-size looseleaf notebook. Photocopy the following pages and punch holes for insertion in the notebook.

The first section of your notebook should list every name (with related information) that you gather through networking. Use the blank "Name of Contact" format on page 47.

The second section should contain an activities report for every day of your 30-day program. You will list all incoming and outgoing calls—names, titles, companies, and phone numbers of everyone you talked with, along with notes about what action you should take next. Use the blank "Day # ____" format on page 48. A filled in sample "Day # ____" format is provided on page 49.

DAY # _____ OF SEARCH   DATE_____

PHONE CALLS	Title	Company	Phone	Address	NEXT STEPS?

PHONE CALLS	Title	Company	Phone	Address	NEXT STEPS?
To hiring authorities					
Dave Mallory	Ch. Eng.	Maril Construction	213/555-4421	557 Old Blue Rd., St. Louis, MO 63118	Call for interview date in 2 wks.
Aubrey Harris	CEO	Harris Medical	213/444-3221	PO Box 417, Kirkwood, MO 62117	Polite but "can't see anyone now"
and so on . . .					
To networking sources					
Greg Maloney-Schultz	Pres.	Avery Construction	208/888-4321		Call Bill Hagen/friend 203/888-5555
					"good info on industry"
Tom Dolfi		Kiwanis Club	208/888-1234		Call Mary Hill/former boss 273-6666
					"looking for Mech. Eng."
Miscellaneous calls					
LETTERS/RESUMES					
Sue Ledder	Supv.	Lawson Constr.	208/777-4545	517 Longshore, Maplewood, MO 63111	Call her in one week
INTERVIEWS					
Fred LeClair	Pres.	LeClair Materials	208/555-1231	207 Filmore Ave., St. Louis, MO 63211	He is "interested—but my sal. req
					a little high"—negotiate?

SEVEN

Using Research to

Find—and Get—Jobs

> - *Photocopy 60 Job Prospect Cards from the end of this section.*
> - *Find the best public or private library in your community.*

I asked an indifferent copywriter what books he had read about advertising. He told me that he had not read any; he preferred to rely on his own intuition. "Suppose," I asked, "your gall-bladder has to be removed this evening. Will you choose a surgeon who has read some books on anatomy and knows where to find your gall-bladder, or a surgeon who relies on his intuition? Why should our clients be expected to bet millions of dollars on your intuition?"

—DAVID OGILVY, *OGILVY ON ADVERTISING*

Personnel directors say an astonishing number of job hunters know little about the company where they plan to work. They come in saying they are anxious to join the staff, but they don't say why. They may not know how big the company is, what products or services it sells, or whether it is currently profitable or unprofitable.

In a way, these job searches resemble the story of a little girl who lived in an orphanage. One day she went to a hollow tree in the institution's yard and poked a small white note into the opening. Each day she returned to the tree to see if the note had been removed. Finally a staff member who had been watching her could not stand the suspense. After she had left, he went to the tree and took out the note. It read:

"To whoever finds this, I love you."

Many job hunters are like this little girl. They may broadcast hundreds of letters and resumes across the country that essentially say, "To who ever finds this, give me a job." Usually, like the little girl, they return to their mailbox to find no takers.

But people who take the time to carefully research their chosen industry and companies can create much more compelling and focused cover letters and resumes. During interviews they can quickly establish a common bond with a company because of their shared interests. Their questions can soar above the naive "What do you manufacture?" to touch on the profit concerns of the company.

They may even have "inside" information on the executives who are interviewing them. (Knowing that someone you'll talk to is a golfer, or is involved in local charities, or is a world traveler may seem like unimportant trivia, but it is definitely early conversation fodder that helps build rapport.)

Where does all of this helpful information come from? From the print media (newspapers, magazines, and newsletters) and the public library.

You should subscribe to all daily and weekly papers within a 50-mile radius of your home, including any business newspapers and magazines published in the area. These can be platinum mines of information about organizations that belong on your Job Prospect Cards.

Print a supply of about 60 of these 4″ × 6″ index cards. You can photocopy the form at the end of this section on page 58. Use them to record the information you gather from the print media, from the library, and through networking. Eventually you could complete around 150 of these Job Prospect Cards (a minimum of five per day). Throughout this program we will continue to suggest a number of sources you can consult to complete these cards.

For general information on industry trends, we recommend

national standbys such as *Business Week,* the *Wall Street Journal, Fortune, Forbes,* and *Barron's.* For information about hot smaller companies, read *Inc.* or *Independent Business* magazines. You don't have to subscribe to any of these. All are usually available at your major source of information—the public library.

One of our colleagues, Lawrence Mayran, partner in A. Brown-Olmstead Associates, a public relations firm in Atlanta, Georgia, describes how he uses the library when he's preparing a proposal for a new client. He goes to the Atlanta-Fulton Public Library. Among the facilities available there are a variety of major computer databases that can call up hundreds of periodicals that publish articles written about almost any subject.

Says Mayran, "The library initially provides the equivalent of about $20 worth of search time free of charge on these computers. You can uncover a great deal of search material during this period.

"For example, database printouts of article references to a potential client company and/or its top manager let me go to the library's periodical shelves and read the actual articles. This way I can put together a substantial profile of the manager—for example, his or her achievements in business and the community, his or her special interests, such as golf, tennis, or charity work—as well as information about the company's management style and the like. When I draft the proposal for the targeted company, I can focus the presentation in a way that has a better chance of appealing to the manager."

Choose the library you use with some care. A given branch may be limited in its directories, computers, and microfiche viewers, all of which can greatly speed your research. Try the main library, even if it's a little less convenient. Don't overlook private libraries at universities, at community colleges, and at other education centers. Many are free to the local community or accessible for a nominal fee. Placement services at schools are often virtual warehouses of employment information and local company profiles. They are always open to alumni—and often to you, too, if you just ask in a friendly way. Most people genuinely want to help someone who is earnestly looking for work.

Get to know the reference librarians. Tell them that you are starting a campaign to get a job and ask for their recommendations. If they seem knowledgeable and helpful, stick with them, and thank them profusely when they come up with new sources or ways to investigate companies.

Take a trial run of the library. Become familiar with how and where the various directories are stored, as you will be using them frequently. Ask about publications that list federal job vacancies. Most libraries also have telephone directories from major U.S. cities and state capitals. Some have microfiches of job listings from the state employment office. Use any computer facilities available to the public and check the availability and costs of copying facilities.

DIRECTORIES AND OTHER PRINTED SOURCES

Here's an example of how to use the directories and books we think you will find most helpful:

First, check to see if the company you're interested in is publicly owned. That's easy. Consult the stock listings of any large newspaper, such as the *Wall Street Journal* or the *New York Times.* Every company listed on the New York Stock Exchange, Amex, or NASDAQ market listings is a publicly traded company.

If you don't see the company, it could be a division, subsidiary, or affiliate of one of the major companies. To check the corporate parent of an organization, consult the annual *Directory of Corporate Affiliations* (National Register Publishing Company), or try *America's Corporate Families* (Dun & Bradstreet), another annual publication.

Once you have the name and corporate lineage of a publicly traded company, look at the following directories. Ask the reference librarian if any of these directories and other sources of corporate information are available on computer databases that are available to the public.

Million Dollar Directory (annual, Dun & Bradstreet). This is an excellent source of information about 160,000 of the largest public and private companies. You can quickly find such information as number of employees, annual sales, and principal corporate officers.

Thomas Register of American Manufacturers (annual, Thomas Publishing Co.). This massive reference is available in 20 volumes, with basic information on 150,000 American manufacturers. The listings are particularly helpful when you want to identify the types of products each company sells. The names of major corporate officers are also listed.

Standard & Poor's Register of Corporations, Directors and Executives (annual, Standard & Poor's Corporation). This directory covers more than 45,000 of the better-known companies. Volume One provides company addresses and names of top officers. An index volume lists companies by product category and geographic location, which is very useful when you are looking for organizations in your commuting zone.

Ward's Business Directory of U.S. Private and Public Companies (annual, Gale Research, Inc.) This book has data on more than 100,000 large companies. One particularly useful feature is a ranking of companies by sales within an industry. There's also a listing of a company's chief competitors and its current share of the market.

To identify the hot new growth companies, check:

Moody's Manuals (annual, with weekly or semiweekly updates; Moody's Investors Service). This is an excellent general source of information on major companies in terms of their history, locations, products sold, etc. The eight titles in the series include financial data for up to seven years so that you can instantly track an organization's growth. You can also check information about municipalities—helpful data if you are interested in working for local government.

Standard & Poor's Corporation Records (annual, updated daily; Standard & Poor's Corporation). This directory is easy to use. Corporations are listed alphabetically, with recent financial data and brief company profiles.

Also see *Standard Stock Reports* (quarterly, Standard & Poor's Corporation) and *Value Line Investment Survey* (weekly, Value Line, Inc.). These publications are written primarily from an investor's point of view but can provide current news about corporate changes that could indicate hiring activity (such as new plant openings and new product introductions).

If you want to review current articles written about the organizations for your Job Prospect Cards or about key executives in your industry specifically, look at the *Business Periodicals Index* (monthly, H.W. Wilson Co.). It lists articles that appear in about 350 English-language magazines. Many journalists use this source to gather information for their articles. Ask if this index is available on the library computer as an on-line database.

For a fast read of current news affecting companies, look at the *Predicasts F&S Index United States* (weekly, Predicasts, Inc), also available as an on-line database in some libraries.

Trade associations in your industry can be great sources of help, information, and sometimes even job leads. To find out how to contact them, see the *Encyclopedia of Associations* (annual, Gale Research, Inc.).

For the names of trade journals and newsletters, see *Ulrich's International Periodicals Directory* (R.R. Bowker, International) or *Gale Directory of Publications and Broadcast Media* (annual, Gale Research, Inc.). Write to every publication in your industry and request a sample copy and subscription rates. Subscribe to those that offer the most comprehensive information and/or classified help-wanted ads.

Information about privately owned companies in your area can be harder, but not impossible, to find. Start with the *AT&T Business to Business Yellow Pages* and your local telephone company Yellow Pages. They can provide company names and addresses in your industry. Advertisements in these books can give you some information about the companies' products or services.

For information about larger privately owned firms, review the *Directory of Leading Private Companies* (annual, National Register Publishing Company). All states and many cities have business directories.

If you would like to get the names of companies and key executives, check the Yellow Pages for mailing-list brokers. You can buy this information on mailing labels or on a PC computer disk. One of these disks could help you set up most of your Job Prospect Cards, adding executive names and addresses, and then address envelopes and letters for you.

Other Sources of Information

As invaluable as the library is to the job seeker, there are still other sources of information about job prospects. One of the most important is your personal visit to the company you'd like to work for. Consider yourself a reporter on assignment to learn all you can about that organization during your visit.

You could start right in the company's lobby. How do the corporate executives dress? Many companies have what seems to be an unwritten dress code. When you dress up to their standards for your interviews, you will already seem to fit right in.

You can often gain access to the company's inner offices by asking the receptionist if you can talk with someone in the public relations or investor relations office. Ask for a copy of the annual report and any company sales literature. People who work in these offices are not nearly as tight-lipped as the gatekeepers (secretaries and administrative assistants) who guard access to corporate executives. You can often engage them in conversation, getting valuable clues about the company, including their current hiring activities. You can also ask if they can refer you to recent magazine or newspaper articles about the company. Ask if you can see a copy of the company phone book. Gatekeepers probably won't let you see this book; public relations and investor relations people often will. This gives you an opportunity to write down the names, titles, and telephone extensions of key executives. While you're in the building, visit the personnel department. Many will accept applications from "walk-ins." Ask the receptionist of that department if the company has a job hot line.

Check any bulletin boards that you see. Available openings may be listed on these bulletin boards, primarily for the benefit of current employees who may want to move up the ladder. If no suitable candidate is found for these positions in the company, the personnel department may then start advertising in the help-wanted columns. Send in your application as soon as you see an appropriate job on the bulletin board and you could be first in line for the position.

Think of every visit and phone call to a company as a learning experience.

Other good sources of information for your Job Prospect-Cards: Chambers of Commerce, industrial development authorities (their job is to bring new business into an area, and they sometimes can supply a list of these organizations), and local labor union representatives.

JOB PROSPECT CARD

Name of organization _____

Address _____ City _____

State _____ Zip _____ Phone ( ) _____ Fax ( ) _____

Industry _____

Products/services _____

"Hiring authorities" (starting with the CEO and personnel/human resources director)

	Title	Phone ext.
1.		
2.		
3.		
4.		
5.		
6.		
7.		
8.		
9.		
10.		

Photocopy this page and cut to create copies of this card.

Expanding Your Network

> • *Recruit a Board of Advisers that can provide advice and information.*
> • *Develop several networking "scripts" that help you get past executives' gatekeepers.*

Two friends meet at a backyard barbecue. After a few minutes of neighborhood talk, one says:

"Mary, I don't know if you've heard. I had been working as head of purchasing at Dalcon's Department Store for about five years, but they let me go last week."

"Bill, that's terrible! What are you going to do?"

"Well, I've started my job search already. Could you let me know if you hear of any job openings?"

This is one concept of networking. And it's *all wrong*.

Mary can provide sympathy, but it's highly unlikely that she would know of any openings for purchasing agents with department store experience. Because she's been put under the pressure of a question she can't answer, she will probably give the standard response: "I'll certainly let you know if I hear of anything." She may then promptly forget this conversation.

Effective networking today must be much more targeted and systematic. Each day you select certain people to contact in person, by phone, or by mail. Your first priority is to contact hiring authorities directly. Your second priority is to talk with people who can provide you with information about certain industries or companies or provide referrals to others who can. If they also happen to know of specific job leads, that's a bonus.

The first type of contact could be called "hard" networking. This is the kind of personal communication that can put you to work in the shortest possible time. We recommend you spend at least 60 percent of a search day making these contacts.

The second type of contact that provides information and referrals is "soft" networking among friends, relatives, neighbors, etc. This is best done during evening hours and weekends. This is also the time to identify those people who will provide the most enthusiastic personal references for you. Save your precious work-week hours for "hard" networking.

Here are two ways you can make networking more productive.

Board of Advisers

Appoint a Board of Advisers to help you. You don't have to use that formal a title, of course. What you want to do is to follow the pattern of President Bill Clinton in his successful drives first for the governorship in Arkansas and later for the presidency of the United States. He systematically developed a group of friends who could provide him with advice when he needed it.

You can do the same. Consider which of your friends could provide useful advice in your job search. These could include a former co-worker who is knowledgeable about your industry, a United Way volunteer who has come in contact with many executives in town, a minister, priest, or rabbi. Call each of them and ask if they would be willing to serve as your advisers for the next month of your job search. Don't pressure them by asking them to help you find a job. All you want is their counsel and any suggestions as to whom you might contact. Many people will be flattered by your request. Send each of them a note of thanks and a copy of your resume for their comments.

Call them once a week or so to report on your progress. Now they have a built-in stake in helping "their" candidate and will be more attuned during the month to things that they see and hear. Each of these people would also make ideal references because they are already committed to your cause. This system *works*. Ask President Clinton or any friends of his.

SAMPLE SCRIPTS

Develop several sample "scripts" when you make hard networking calls. Senior executives at major corporations usually are guarded by a ring of gatekeepers (secretaries and administrative assistants). Their *job* is to protect the time of the executive by deflecting or diverting any unnecessary calls, correspondence, or personal visits from people the executive does not know or regularly do business with.

If you call a CEO and say you are looking for a job, the gatekeeper's almost knee-jerk reaction will be to refer you to the personnel department. That's why you should take an indirect route. Try these scenarios.

• *Use a name.* If your various soft networking contacts have referred you to an executive, always use that contact's name: "I'd like to speak to Ms. Waters. Mrs. Jefferies of Old Dominion Bank suggested I call her."

• *Request information about a client or a competitor.*

This is perfectly legitimate when you are doing your regular research on an industry or company. "I'd like to speak to Ms. Waters—in confidence. I am gathering some information for a report about (name of competitor)." Many senior executives will take this call. After all, you could be a potential customer!

Before you reach the executive, set several goals for your conversation and write them on a piece of paper you keep in front of you during the call. You could even write a short script with questions. Remember:

• You want more information about the company.

• You would appreciate the names of other individuals in that organization whom you could talk with. (As soon as the executive refers you to another person, your next call gains the immediate clout of "the president suggested I call you.") These calls almost always breach the next gatekeeper's wall.

• You would like to come in for a brief (15-minute) informational interview about the company. At this point you can say you are doing this because you are looking for jobs in that industry and want to gather as much information as possible before applying. Asking for information rather than a job takes the pressure off the executive. Most people not in the midst of a crisis are willing to stop and talk about their work.

Don't memorize any script. You could come off like one of those evening callers who sounds like a mechanical robot: "Our window crew will be in your neighborhood tomorrow. Can they stop by to give you a free estimate on . . . hello? . . . hello?" Instead use the script only as an outline to be sure you've met your main objectives.

Job fairs, trade shows, and industry seminars can be fertile hunting grounds for the person who is networking. You will have very little time to talk with individual executives. Try to ask a question about their company or the industry in general (such as trade with Mexico) and collect their business cards.

Then on the next day you have another way to leapfrog the gatekeeper.

"I was speaking with Ms. Walters yesterday. I am calling for some more information about the effects on profits of the Mexican trade practices that we discussed."

Networking and the Hidden Job Market

Here's another example from our experiences in hiring people.

Week one: A magazine's advertising is steadily increasing, and the editor requires more editorial material to balance the ads.

Weeks two and three: The pressure increases. The editor requests authorization from management to hire an additional staffer.

Week four: The requisition request comes back "approved."

Week five: The job requirements are outlined and sent to personnel.

Week six: The job opening is sent to several key headhunters, and an ad is placed in the Sunday newspaper.

Weeks seven and eight: Over 200 people apply.

Look at that timetable again. For almost five weeks, that job opening was in the "hidden" job market. What would have happened at any point during those five weeks if one of our colleagues had said, "I know of someone I worked with before who could be good for that job."

That person would have been called in. Because the need was urgent, he or she would have stood a good chance of being hired if qualified. And that's exactly what happens, more often than not. Most people who hire others are leery of hiring strangers. They would greatly prefer the reassurance of hiring someone recommended by a third party whom they trust.

That's what today's networking is all about. You spread word-of-mouth advertising about yourself—your interest in the company, your skills, the added value you can bring to the company. Then others carry the ball for you.

THE POWER OF NETWORKING

One way to visualize the enormous power of networking is to try to solve the "lily puzzle."

One day you plant a lily in a pond. That lily has the ability to reproduce itself in just 24 hours. By the second day there are two lilies in the pond, and so on. By the thirtieth day, the pond is completely filled with lilies. On what day of that month was the pond *half* filled?

( ) Day 15
( ) Day 20
( ) Day 29

If you checked the last choice, you would be right. If you didn't, reread the puzzle and you'll see why.

This is a pretty good analogy for networking. Every time you contact someone in a memorable way, he or she may tell others about your ideas or availability. They in turn may reach others. If you spread the word among many within a specific industry or company, you dramatically increase the exponential power of networking.

It also reveals one of the problems with networking—it often works in invisible ways. Job hunters may abandon networking because they believe it doesn't work. However, they might be abandoning networking on the twenty-ninth day, right before it doubles in dimension.

Networking is not brain surgery. It's simply being friendly,

showing real interest in an industry or a company and its executives, and exchanging useful ideas.

This could lead to the ultimate in networking—when someone in a company says to a boss who's looking for help, "I know
somebody."

Business leaders want to help—if you remove the pressure.

Many people are afraid to network among strangers,
either because of shyness or fear of rejection.

We recently asked about 50 top business leaders at
a Rotary Club meeting, "How many of you would respond to a call from a stranger inquiring about jobs in
your company?" Only about 10 held up their hands.
Several explained they didn't know of any immediate
jobs and didn't want to waste the time of the caller or
themselves.

We changed the question: "How many of you would
be willing to meet with a stranger who called asking for
information about your company or industry?" *Almost
every person in the room raised their hand.*

Three keys for fast networking

Marcia Layton recently wrote us with an example of
how fast networking can sometimes work.

"I recently left Kodak to start my own business and
since then have been offered several full-time and part-
time positions. The first offer came two days after I
left my job. It was a free-lance assignment at a local
bank, which came through my network of colleagues at
organizations in the Rochester, New York, area. I'm a
member of several professional organizations and am
on the board of directors of one, so I have frequent
contact with senior-level managers. The free-lance as-

signment came through a contact on the board of directors. Other offers have come my way as a result of my name being mentioned to managers looking to hire someone with my specific skills."

Ms. Layton offers these personal networking tips:

"Get involved in local professional organizations, and make every effort to attend meetings to network with other members. Join committees, where you can get to know a smaller group of colleagues very well.

"Try to be a resource for other people. Instead of contacting someone to ask for something, be on the lookout for ways that you can help that person. And don't expect something in return!

"Get involved in at least one charity or nonprofit organization that you are interested in. You will meet an entirely different crowd of people who may ultimately be able to direct you to someone who has a job opening."

Finding the Best

Employment Agencies

- *Send a letter and resume to at least 100 agencies and headhunters.*
- *Select two good local agents to represent you (and—if your search is national—several who specialize in your industry or occupational specialty).*
- *Register in at least one electronic job bank.*

A QUICK BRIEFING

There are more than 10,000 employment or recruiting companies in the United States. They can be roughly divided into four categories.

The first can be called *general employment agents,* although some specialize in finding employment in particular industries or for particular occupational specialties. They usually work on contingency, with no fee due until a job has been found and accepted. They then bill the job hunter or the hiring company. We strongly recommend choosing agencies with the latter approach because the fee can be a large percentage of your first year's salary.

The second broad category is *executive search firms* (often called by a name most of them thoroughly dislike, *headhunters*). These companies are paid by organizations to fill specific job openings. They are retained, which means they get paid by the companies for their services whether or not they successfully find candidates. They are primarily looking for executives on the upper end of the annual salary scale, starting at a minimum of $60,000 to $70,000. Their preference: high-profile executives, usually already employed.

The third category is *employment counseling firms.* Some of these advertise exactly like employment agencies. They may even promise jobs. Many are excellent, but some are run by charlatans and buffoons, passing out ''same-old, same-old'' employment information and charging high fees for their clichés. Paul Plawin reported on many of these scams during his years as careers editor of Kiplinger's *Changing Times* magazine. Among his findings: ''Some of these companies advertise jobs or pretend to be employment agencies. When they lure people to the door, they try to sign them up for expensive job counseling. Often these companies have no jobs at all and never actively seek jobs for their clients.''

The fourth category includes *state and local employment offices* that offer free services to job seekers. Some are now offering highly sophisticated new electronic search services for executives as well as blue-collar workers. Others are badly underfunded and resemble old bus depots furnished with scarred desks. You won't know until you visit your local office in person.

Advance Research

Before contacting any employment agency, do a little research.

If you're an executive looking for a midlevel position, your best bet is general employment agencies, particularly those that specialize in your industry and occupational specialty.

Ask friends and relatives about their personal experiences with local agencies. Call company personnel or human resources departments and ask which employment agencies they work with. (While you're on the phone with them, ask about current employment opportunities at their company. Make every call count *twice.*)

Then send a letter and resume to local and national employment agents. You can generally expect a high response rate to this letter, usually greater than 10 percent. Conduct this research and correspondence the week before you start your 30-day job program.

Call local agents that meet your requirements. Arrange for a face-to-face meeting with a job counselor and treat this meeting just as you would a regular job interview. This is a good opportunity for you to ask for feedback about your resume and how you come across in person. Read any agency application form with care. Some of these forms are also contracts. Don't sign anything until you've read the fine print. You are looking for an agent *whose fee is paid by the employer.*

SOME SEARCH CRITERIA

Look for agencies that have been in business at least two years. In that time they should have cultivated a wide circle of employers. Another plus is membership in the National Association of Personnel Consultants (NAPC). If you want the brightest consultant in the place, ask for one with CPC accreditation. Those letters stand for Certified Personnel Consultant and indicate that the individual is a thorough professional who has graduated from a rigorous training program.

Don't register with more than two agencies locally—when an agency job counselor learns from an employer that he has received three or four of your resumes from different employment agencies, the counselor will usually stop working for you.

If you are looking for a top-level job and are accustomed to earning top dollar, it can be worthwhile to contact executive recruiters. You will get less of a response from this group to any mailing you do. They often will call or write you only if they are currently looking for someone with your qualifications based on an assignment from one of their clients. You can increase this response rate by sending letters only to those recruiters who are looking for people in your industry, occupational specialty, and salary bracket. A good source of this information is the *Directory of Executive Recruiters,* published by Kennedy Publications. The names given in the directory are also available on mailing labels; for more information, call 603-585-2200. For a targeted list of contingency and retained employment agencies in specific industry categories, you can contact the National Job Campaigning Resource Center, at 904-235-3733.

When you are interviewed by an executive recruiter, respond

to that person exactly as you would to a prospective employer. He or she represents the employer and will usually write an objective report to the client that summarizes your qualifications, how you conduct yourself, and how well you communicate.

Visit your state and local employment offices. Some are becoming increasingly sophisticated in their job-search techniques, more and more geared to the needs of the growing number of white collar workers looking for work. Computers are now available to take you through self-guided programs that will help you identify available jobs in such categories as "managerial and professional," "sales and related fields," and "manufacturing, construction, transportation, and related." Some employment offices also have microfiche viewers that let you spool through hundreds of jobs available in other areas. These offices should be your first stop when looking for federal, state, or local government jobs. Some of their out-of-state job information may be dated (one month or more), but many employment offices have solved this problem by developing interstate computer networks. State and local employment offices offer specialized help to former military personnel, often with certain counselors designated to help veterans translate their service experience into civilian-related job skills.

When you register with an employment office or agency be sure to check with your job counselor every two weeks about any activity. Don't pressure them. Just keep your name at the center of his or her awareness.

In addition to registering with employment agencies, we recommend you sign up with at least one job bank. These computerized services keep your resume in an electronic data bank and then match your qualifications with the job requirements of the job bank's corporate clients. One caution: Some job banks make most of their money from registering job hunters, not finding jobs. Look for job banks that have achieved national prominence and gained corporate clients who regularly use their services.

Three nationally known job banks are:

- **kiNexus\Adease,** one of the largest with 175,000 resumes in its data bank. Annual registration fee, $30. For more information call 800-828-0422.

- **Job Bank USA,** specializing in technical and professional jobs with 22,000 resumes in its database. The annual registration fee is $30. A spokesperson said, "Four hundred employers use our services." For more information call, 800-296-1872.
- **SkillSearch,** with 30,000 resumes in its database. "We have 300 employers as clients and average twenty-five to thirty job searches of our database each week." The registration fee is $65 for the first year, with a $15 annual maintenance fee thereafter. For more information, call 800-258-6641.

Because of the growing uncertainties of the job market, some people keep their resumes registered at these job banks even after they have found a job. This means they are always in the marketplace if a better job develops. However, be sure to notify the job bank of the name of your new employer when you get a job. You do *not* want the job bank to send your resume to your current employer!

TEN

Responding Effectively to Help-Wanted Ads

> - *Collect sample copies of all local newspapers, news-letters, and magazines in your targeted geographic area.*
> - *Subscribe to those with the most useful job-hunting news and recruitment ads.*
> - *Follow some simple techniques to increase your number of favorable responses.*

Many people still get jobs the old-fashioned way—they answer a help-wanted ad. The problem today is that competition has become so intense that up to 2,000 people (or more) may respond to an ad for a high-paying position or one placed by a well-known company.

TRICKS OF THE TRADE

Fortunately, you can use some tricks of the ad-answering trade to improve the odds of your being called in for an interview.

- When the advertised job seems just right for you, give your application special treatment that will make it stand out from the crowd.

     Target your response directly to the text of the ad. On one side of a sheet of paper write every job requirement stated in the ad. Then on the other side write your past jobs, skills, and experiences that most closely match those requirements. (Here your

Life Experience Cards, as explained in Chapter Four, will prove invaluable.)

Do your research on the company.

Now write a cover letter and resume targeted directly at that position.

Most of your competitors simply won't spend the time and effort to do this. From a time-management standpoint, you *can't* do it for every job application. Sometimes you must send out your standard cover letter and resume. But when you really want a particular job, go the extra mile.

Be sure to answer every point raised in the ad, except the one that says, "State your salary requirements." If you name a figure that is too high or too low, your application could be rejected immediately. (A low salary figure may make them think you're not qualified.) Instead give a salary range and emphasize that you are willing to negotiate, but that you are primarily interested in finding a position in which you can grow.

- Send a *second* application to the same company five days later. *It should be an identical application that makes no reference to the first one you sent.* When stacks of resumes arrive on a Monday morning, a corps of junior executives may make a preliminary screening. Your second application, arriving a little later, may now get more attention because the pile has shrunk. It also may be read by a second person who has a more favorable response than the first person who reviewed it.

- *Make a follow-up call.* If no person or department is listed in the ad, call the company's personnel or human resources department. Many people don't do this for fear of being considered "pests." But, pest or not, you may force them to take a second look at your resume (just when they're in a crunch to hire someone).

- If the company placing a large ad is in your industry, send your application to them *even if they don't seem to be looking for someone with your occupational specialty.* The ad indicates that they are expanding, and while today they may need only chemical engineers, two weeks from now they may need several new computer technicians to handle the work generated by those new engineers.

- Check help-wanted ads that are about six months old (usually available on microfiche at your library). Six months is a normal try-out period for people hired from ads. Your application could arrive just when some of those people have been fired or moved on to greener pastures.

• Placing situation-wanted classified ads in the newspapers is usually a complete waste of money. Most of the responses may even come from people who are *looking* for work. However, we have known executives who've gotten jobs by placing small display ads about themselves on newspaper business and sports pages.

Now your goal setting will begin to pay off. You have already decided to search for jobs locally and/or nationally and/or internationally. This decision will directly affect which help-wanted ads you should check regularly.

For Local Recruitment Ads

Take out a local map and draw a circle around your home. The radius of this circle is determined by how far you are willing to commute each day to a job. Mark every community and major neighborhood near or within this circle. Now take the map to the library and obtain the names of every major or neighborhood newspaper in these areas.

Two good reference sources are *Gale Directory of Publications and Broadcast Media* and *Editor and Publisher International Yearbook*.

Show your final list of publications to a reference librarian and ask if he or she knows of any others that should be included. Also ask which are available at the library; this can save you substantial money in subscription costs. Send a postcard to the circulation department of every publication listed in or near your search circle, with the following message: "I am currently looking for a position in your area and may be interested in subscribing to your publication. Would you please send me a sample copy and subscription rates." Order those that look most promising.

You should subscribe immediately (if you haven't done so already) to the major newspaper serving your city or town. Also sign up for daily home delivery (or buy at a nearby convenience store) a newspaper from the largest city in your region (the *New York Times, Baltimore Sun, Chicago Tribune, Los Angeles Times,* etc.).

Most of these carry ads for positions in the surrounding region. You particularly want to get the Sunday editions, which always carry the most ads.

For National Recruitment Ads

Subscribe to the *Wall Street Journal*. (If you're watching your budget, read it free in the library.) Always get the Tuesday edition, which carries the largest concentration of help-wanted ads.

Also subscribe to *National Business Employment Weekly*, which reprints recruitment ads from all four regional editions of the *Wall Street Journal* (800-562-2832; available at newsstands), and to *The National Ad Search*, a weekly that reprints recruitment ads from 72 major newspapers in the United States (800-992-2832).

For a national employment search, you should also obtain newspapers from the cities and regions where you want to settle. The local library usually subscribes to the major national papers.

Contact national professional and trade associations in your industry to request sample copies of their newsletters and other publications. Many carry a limited amount of recruitment advertising. However, their major value to you is to let you track recent developments in the industry or add companies to your job prospect list. For the names and phone numbers of these associations, see the *Encyclopedia of Associations*.

For International Recruitment Ads

The *Wall Street Journal* and major U.S. newspapers frequently carry help-wanted ads placed by overseas companies. Other international newspapers such as the *Financial Times* of London and the *International Herald Tribune* also carry recruitment ads. For a list of newspapers, newsletters, and magazines published in specific foreign cities, see *Ulrich's International Periodicals Directory*.

Job Hunters, Beware

Some ads in help-wanted sections are scams placed by companies preying on the unemployed. Here are two examples:

Job information offered by 900 number. The ad offers employment in glamorous jobs in television, marketing, modeling, etc. You call the 900 number and may be charged up to $5 for each minute—for general information that is usually available free of charge in any public library. A new variation has cropped up recently. You call a toll-free 800 number listed in the ad and are immediately referred to a 900 number.

There are some legitimate 900 employment information numbers. (Even the U.S. government offers one that we discuss in Part IV of this book—see Job-Hunting Project #33.) But they are few and far between.

High-paying jobs overseas—in Australia, South America, Europe, etc. That's what the help-wanted ads promise. But you have to pay a fee. A consumer advocate decided to test some of these numbers recently. She responded to a "top overseas jobs" ad in a Florida newspaper. The "employment agent" on the line asked her what type of position she wanted. She said that she wanted to be a truck driver in Rio, but she did have this one little problem. She had never driven anything larger than a Ford Mustang. No problem at all, said the agent. She could go to work almost immediately driving a truck in Rio for $50,000 a year—after she paid her employment fee.

Developing Resumes That

Are Read

> • *A good resume is an absolute must in a job search.*
> • *Use your Life Experience Cards to customize resumes for specific job openings.*

As you've read in earlier chapters, the resume, cover letter, and interview are absolute musts in a job search.

You may hear or read that the resume is old hat or even out of style now. Follow that advice at your peril. Everyone needs a resume. You don't have to call it a resume, of course. Call it your personal information brochure, if you like. But you definitely need one. You'll use this document just as businesses and entrepreneurs use a concise sales and marketing flyer. In your case, it will give an at-a-glance picture of your professional background.

It may have been a while since you last wrote your resume. Like anything else you haven't done in a long spell, crafting a good resume will appear daunting. You're bound to have questions like:

- What goes into a resume?
- How many pages should it be?
- Can I make photocopies or should I pay for a supply of printed copies?
- Should I use colored paper?

Creating a resume is not a snap for anyone who isn't a skilled writer. But if you follow the tips and the examples of documents we give you here, you'll be a pro in no time.

First, let's review what your resume has to do, and what most employers expect it to look like.

A resume alone won't get you the job. Face-to-face contact with employers is what gets you the job. That's how an employer can get a real sense of who you are, how you handle yourself, and what it would be like to have you as an employee. Getting that interview is the major first accomplishment in a successful job hunt. And a good resume can help you get that far. That's what a resume really is—a door opener. It's a professional calling card, your personal sales brochure, a concise professional profile of You, Inc.

There are resumes that give a good impression of who you are. And there are resumes that are merely lists of jobs. Some people are said to be nothing *but* a resume—that is, they boast a long string of impressive job titles, but character or personality is lacking. There seems to be nothing beyond the titles. That's not the kind of resume you want nor the kind of person your prospective employer wants to hire.

You want a resume that will reveal more about you than simply the jobs you've held. You want to create one that will separate you from the dozens, sometimes hundreds, of other equally qualified applicants vying for the same job.

WHAT TO INCLUDE

Start with a blank sheet of paper—or a blank screen on your personal computer—and center your name and address and phone numbers right up there at the top. Make sure you provide phone numbers where you can be reached during the business day and in the evening. If you list only a home phone, have an answering machine operating 24 hours a day. Check this machine every time you go out, even for short periods. Return calls promptly.

Now review all of your Life Experience Cards. Group your cards under different headings, such as "work experiences," "education," "awards, special achievements," "volunteer activities," etc. Each stack of cards will then help you write different sections of the resume. For example, as you write the resume section on "work experiences," you can refer to the cards to list and describe your work history, beginning with your present position and working back to your first job since leaving school.

Notice that we didn't tell you to list an "objective," as many resume books suggest. It could guarantee that your resume often won't be read at all. Putting some narrowly focused objective at the top of a resume pigeonholes you and gives the person reading it good reason to discard it right away if your "objective" doesn't exactly fit the jobs the reader needs to fill.

As you begin to describe your work experiences, don't just list each job, your title, your employer, and the dates you worked there. Also describe in brief your responsibilities, the number of people you supervised, and one or two of your significant accomplishments in the position. Be sure to avoid generalities. Use statistics and hard facts. For example, "Led 14-person sales force that increased gross revenues by 43 percent over a two-year period," or "Reorganized the department, increasing output by 12 percent over the previous year." Use examples that are most relevant to the type of position you are looking for. This information should be at your fingertips if you have listed it on your Life Experience Cards.

You may wonder what to put down as a current job when you're out of work. And you are correct in assuming that an unexplained gap of time raises questions, rings bells, raises flags, and calls for an explanation. *So don't leave such a gap.* You may not be working for the company that laid you off, but remember that you *are* working for You, Inc. You're self-employed and looking for contract work or a return to employment by a larger firm.

So, if you are an engineer, for instance, as your current position put "consulting engineer." If you're a lawyer or accountant, you're a lawyer or accountant, of course, in private practice and looking for a corporate spot. If you're in sales, you are a sales or marketing consultant. Other common terms for self-employed individuals: training director, writer-editor, computer analyst, management consultant.

You've heard the snide put-down interpretation that consultants are really just people who are out of work. Don't let that keep you from being a consultant at least in your resume. What do you think is smarter: to leave a noticeable gap in your career track that signals "out of work" or to identify yourself as a consultant or similar variation of sole proprietor? In today's business world, consultants and independent contractors often seem to outnumber employed staff people. In fact, if your psyche can tolerate the wavy lines of a consultant's income stream, you might make a very good living being one. In any event, being in business for yourself is far too common to be a cover for an out-of-work klutz. Use your title on your business cards, too.

If you've completed a couple of projects in the past 18 months, you can cite them on your resume, or list some names of clients, or just describe the nature of the work you've completed for several unnamed clients.

When you take the information from your Life Experience Cards and transfer it to your resume, write it down in clear language, much as you would tell someone about it. Write in a conversational style. Don't use unnecessarily big words or a lot of jargon. Direct and to the point is best. Use phraseology like that in the model resumes that follow. For instance, "Directed the work of 16 computer operators" is a sign of a more organized mind than something like "Was responsible for supervision of all of the department's networked PC operators, which included 16 individuals."

Heed the advice of Yale writing professor William Zinser, who wrote in his book *On Writing Well,* "Strip every sentence to its cleanest component. Every word that serves no function, every long word that could be a short word, every adverb that carries the same meaning that's already in the verb, every passive construction that leaves the reader unsure of who is doing what— these are the thousand and one adulterants that weaken the strength of a sentence. And they usually occur, ironically, in proportion to education and rank."

As you move a decade or more into the past in listing your work experience, it's not as important to elaborate on job-related achievements, unless they were unique or spectacular. Use the inverted-pyramid style of writing a resume, putting more detail at the top and tapering off at the bottom as you list your early experiences, when your jobs were certainly not as involved or eventful.

Having completed the review of your work experience, you

can cite your education. Note your degree or degrees and where you got them. Also cite any other significant training you've completed—for instance, at professional workshops or seminars in your field. Depending on your field and the nature of the job you are seeking, this is where you could also note your working knowledge of computer software.

That's the kernel of a resume—your past work experience and accomplishments and your educational background. That's what a prospective employer needs to know to size you up on paper. Your past performance is the best indication of future promise and may determine whether an employer calls you in for an interview.

Other information you might want to include in your resume—if you have room for it and if it tells something about your character and professional standing—is membership in professional societies, trade associations, or community organizations, and any offices you've held in these groups. Participation in these organizations can speak of your leadership abilities. If you headed up a fund drive for the local civic orchestra or served on the city school board, these facts say something about your management skills. If you are customizing a resume for a particularly important job and your research has uncovered the fact that the CEO or other company officials have been leaders in a United Way drive, you certainly would want to include any similar volunteer experience you may have had.

But don't overload your resume with such material. Remember, your resume should never be more than two pages long. One page is the ideal; two pages is the max! Push beyond that limit and you risk setting yourself up as someone who can't get to the point quickly.

Here are more things you should not include in your resume:

- *Don't list references.* If employers want them, they'll ask you for names, addresses, and phone numbers at a later stage of the process. In our litigious society, what references do or don't say to an inquiring employer can end up as the subject of a lawsuit, so some employers are very careful about consulting references. Let the employer take the lead on this.

- *Don't indicate salary figures*—either what you made at previous jobs or what you hope to make at your next one.
- *Don't load up your resume with strictly personal information* that is in no way related to your work or career. Data like your age and marital status are unnecessary. Employers may risk lawsuits by disgruntled applicants if such facts are taken into consideration in hiring, so most of them would rather not have this information. Also, your hobbies and personal interests outside of work aren't pertinent in a resume. (Of course, if you happen to know that the company sponsors major golf tournaments and you once won an amateur golf title, you could slip this into your cover letter.)
- *Never indicate reasons for leaving jobs.* There can only be three reasons—you left to take a better job, you were laid off, or you got fired. Let the progression of jobs in your resume paint a picture of advancement in your field. If one or more of your career moves was the result of a layoff or firing, there is absolutely nothing to be gained by bringing it up. Period. If there are gaps in your progression that you think may need explaining, wait until the job interview to do that if the employer brings it up.

Now Your Resume May Be Read by a Computer!

Syndicated careers columnist Joyce Lain Kennedy reports that many major companies and executive recruiters are tossing out filing cabinets and replacing them with computerized in-house applicant tracking systems. These systems file resumes and retrieve those that match specific job descriptions. (Early in the Clinton administration, the White House used such a computerized system, Resumix, to organize resumes from thousands of job hunters.)

When retrieving resumes these systems usually look for "key words" that characterize the applicant's skills and achievements. For an accounting manager, the computer may look for words such as "supervisor," "manager," and "BS, Accounting." For a salesperson: "BS/BA," "exceeded quota," and "will travel."

To cover all your electronic bases—especially if you know the company to which you are applying screens resumes by computer—add a summary of key words in a brief paragraph right at the top of your resume (under your name and address). Tag it simply: "Key Word Index."

Spend several days writing your resume, more if you need to. Put it aside for a day or so and then return to it with a fresh eye. It's a good idea to put together several resumes—one general-purpose resume that you'll use in most circumstances, and one or more special-focus resumes that you can later customize for particular jobs.

FORMAT AND APPEARANCE

Chronological Order

There are two basic resume styles. In one you present a narrative of your work or life experience in reverse *chronological order,* starting with your present job and working back through earlier jobs. This is the most common type of resume, used by most job seekers today, and we've provided a sample on page 85.

Functional Format

In the other style, you organize your work or life experience by three or four different skill areas. For example, if you have held positions in sales and marketing as well as in general administration and communications, you could group your previous jobs and companies under these functional headings without regard to the chronology of your employment history. With this *functional* format, you may be able to target a specific kind of job you want even more specifically than with the chronological resume. The functional format also may show off your versatility, if you have been successful in two or three or more areas of work over the years. There's a sample of this resume type on page 87.

Which should you use? That depends on your background and goals. Both styles can be effective. Use the one that best presents you and your work history. You might want to prepare resumes in several formats to cover all your bases. Some resumes are a combination of both formats.

Don't lose sight of the fact that your resume should be a quick read. Keep it to two pages max. Resist your urge to lay out your whole career in multiple pages. How do you feel about paper that comes across your desk? We *all* know what happens to overly long reports and memos. Remember that the appearance of your resume is also important. It *must* look good—after all, it may be competing with hundreds of others for every job you go after. Yours doesn't have to be the fanciest or most unique in the pile, but it had better look like one of the best. That means it should at least be printed, not simply typewritten and photocopied. If you don't have access to a laser printer that can produce a sharp copy with some attractive typeface styles, take the computer disk with your resume to an instant print shop or resume service agency that can produce a quality copy for you. And, of course, if you don't have access to a word-processing program on a personal computer, take your resume draft to a word-processing service agency and have them turn it into a professional-looking document.

Before the final copy of your resume is printed, you should have proofread it several times to eliminate spelling or spacing errors and awkward or incorrect grammar. Sometimes we have trouble seeing our own mistakes, so have a friend or colleague proofread your resume, too.

If you are not completely satisfied with the final result of your effort, hire a professional resume writer. They are listed in the Yellow Pages and often advertise their services at the front of the help-wanted section of your local newspaper. How do you know if they're good? Contact several resume writers and look at samples of their work. Do the resumes they've done impress you with their content and style, or do they read like a canned, by-the-numbers document? Discuss the writer's fee. Does it include revisions? You don't want to be surprised by any unexpected costs.

One caution: Some career advisers recommend against having resumes prepared by a third party. The reason is that in an interview session you could be asked questions about certain statements in your resume that you are not completely familiar with— since you didn't write them. Any uncertainty you display does not advance your cause.

With your resume in hand, you're now prepared to step up your job-search activity.

A sample of a chronological resume follows on page 85. This lists your work history in order, starting at the top with your current position and listing previous positions in descending order. It is not necessary to show dates of employment, which could work against older candidates.

PAUL B. DOE
116 N. Main Street
Moorland, CA 63185
Home phone 805/229-8700
Fax 805/229-8709

PROFESSIONAL BACKGROUND

Currently

• President, Paul Doe Associates, Moorland, California. Provide customized marketing plans and sales training to companies in the $3 million to $25 million gross sales range. Clients include Playfun Games, Inc., of Los Angeles, Bromwell Investors of Salt Lake City, and the Newsletter Advisory Corporation of Las Vegas.

Previous positions

• Regional Sales Manager, Schulte Tool and Die, Inc., Tampa, Florida. Directed a sales force of 22, which consistently produced over 40 percent of the company's annual gross sales volume (in the $25 million range). Duties included creating operating/sales budgets and formulating marketing/training programs.

• Assistant Sales Manager, Block Engineering Co., Wilton, Connecticut. Directed a staff of four to provide extensive market research support for sales operations for a $61 million gross sales company. Planned research projects, assisted in training sales associates, and prepared quarterly sales reports. Sales staff increased gross sales by 4 percent or greater in each of my six years with the firm.

• Client Representative, South Coast Temps, San Diego, California. Responsible for signing up client companies for temp services. Perfected effective new way to make cold calls. Designed a marketing plan that produced the largest number of sales to new clients in a single quarter.

Background information

• Active in community and professional activities and organizations. Speaker at regional meetings of such groups as the Society of Market Research and the American Sales Roundtable. Member of the National Marketing Society, on the board of the United Way, and former president of the Athens Middle School PTA. Graduate of UCLA, B.S., Economics.

A sample of a functional resume follows on page 87. This type of resume can be most effective when you don't have a number of companies to list in your work history. For example, if you have worked for one company most of your life, this resume allows you to describe the many different areas of the company that you worked in.

PAUL B. DOE
116 N. Main Street
Moorland, CA 63185
Home phone 805/229-8700
Fax 805/229-8709

PROFESSIONAL BACKGROUND

Sales Management

Managing sales has been the major focus of my work with companies such as Playfun Games, Inc. of Los Angeles, Schulte Tool and Die of Salt Lake City, and South Coast Temps in San Diego, California. Have directed sales forces of more than 20 persons; set up training programs for regional and national sales reps. Have led sales teams to improved annual sales gains nine years in a row.

Marketing

The underlying strength of my sales management experience has been my overall marketing knowledge and skills. At Schulte Tool and Die my strategies consistently produced over 40 percent of the company's annual gross sales volume. Designed a marketing plan for South Coast Temps that produced the largest number of new clients in a single quarter.

Market Research

Have solid foundations in the principles and practical applications of market research. With Playfun Games, conducted market research studies that were the basis for direct mail promotions that produced a response rate of better than 3.2 percent.

Background Information

Active in community and professional activities and organizations. Speaker at regional meetings of such groups as the Society of Market Research and the American Sales Roundtable. Member of the National Marketing Society, on the board of the United Way, and former president of the Athens Middle School PTA. Graduate of UCLA, B.S., Economics.

Writing Compelling Cover Letters

> • *Preview your major accomplishments in the letter that accompanies your resume. Use facts about the company to grab attention.*

Develop a good basic letter that you can use for almost all job inquiries and then customize it by adding special paragraphs that you think would be of special interest to a particular company.

You'll need a basic letter to answer help-wanted ads, to write to a CEO of one of your job prospects, to follow up a call to a potential hiring authority, to respond to a lead from a networking associate, or simply to establish your presence with a cold contact. Each of these letters is slightly different, but the core of every letter should include an opening that snags the reader's interest, a statement that identifies who you are and what your strengths are, and a specific action statement, such as "I will call you next Monday to see if I might spend 15 minutes with you during the week."

Your letter should focus like a laser on your target company. Always address your letter to someone at the company who is in a position to hire you. Make certain you have that person's name spelled correctly and that his or her title is accurate. In most cases, you can obtain the name, title, and address of the top manager in the department in which you aspire to work—sales, engineering, information management—with a call to the company switchboard. Be sure to confirm the spelling of the name. If the receptionist asks why you need this information, say you want to send an important letter and you want to be sure you've spelled the name correctly.

There are certain points that you must get across in your letter, so before you start each new letter, you might want to create a simple outline that takes into account specific aspects of the company you are writing to or the position you are seeking. The idea is to customize your letter to best meet the interests and needs of the company.

Right off the dime, introduce yourself and give your reason for writing: You are looking for a job at this company, or you are responding to the company's help-wanted ad (always note where and when the ad you saw was published).

Next mention the reason that you are especially interested in working for this company—for example, they are a major player in your field, or because of their pattern of development. A hiring authority is almost always impressed if you can identify what distinguishes a company from its competitors. (Here's where you can use the research you've collected on your Job Prospect Cards.)

Follow with what *added value* you can bring to the company. This kind of strategic thinking can put you way ahead of job candidates who write the typical "I am interested in the job and believe my abilities and experience are a perfect match for this position" type of letter. Yet don't overplay your added value pitch, and avoid giving the impression that you know the company and its needs better than the person to whom your letter is addressed. Your research should also identify some of the industry's general problems rather than just those of the company to which you are writing. And you can refer to these problems in your letter.

Preview in your letter some of your key accomplishments, which are mentioned in your resume. You might go into a bit more detail in your letter than you have in your resume, giving the material the extra attention appropriate to the target company. Establish your added value in a couple of succinct paragraphs, and move toward a good close. Tell what immediate response you'd like to your letter. Ask for a job interview.

Allow enough time (about one week) for the person you are writing to to respond. Then make a follow-up call to be sure the correspondence was received and to try to initiate a meeting.

Does such follow-up seem natural to you? It should. Isn't that the way you always went after new business for your former company? Follow up on every letter you write. It will give you a creative edge, because most companies want people who are determined and not easily discouraged, yet many job hunters will simply let a letter contact die.

There are a couple of things you want to be sure to avoid in your letters. As in your resume, don't give the impression that you have been out of work and idle. Remember, you are self-employed. Couch your descriptions of accomplishments in the present or immediate past tense. Don't mention salary figures. The purpose of your letter is to make a contact and get an appointment for a face-to-face meeting. There will be more appropriate times to talk about money—such as when an employer says, "We'd like you to come to work for us."

So how do you respond to ads that directly request that you include your salary history or requirements? Just ignore such requests altogether. If your response package is impressive in every other aspect, its lack of salary data should not derail you. A more cautious approach—if you're not comfortable with omitting this information altogether—is to give a salary range that would be acceptable to you. But be certain that you can live with the bottom figure of your range, because why should an employer offer you any more than you've indicated you are willing to accept?

You could note your most recent salary figure, but you should certainly give some indication of the fringes to show the total compensation picture. If you think this figure might scare off a potential employer, you can say that money will not be the deciding factor in your choice of a new job. (And, face it, as absolutely important as money is, it shouldn't be the only reason you take a job.) You might be smart to take the lesser-paying of two jobs offered—if it is the kind of job you really want or the one that you think offers the most growth potential.

SAMPLE COVER LETTER

Much of the language in this sample can easily be adapted to your job field and background.

Here is a list of some points to remember when writing your own cover letter. (The numbers correspond with those of the sample letter on page 92.)

1. Be sure to use the name and title of a hiring authority within the organization. Check the spelling carefully.
2. Identify who you are and why you are writing. This letter is an example of a cold mailing—an unsolicited application to a company. If you are responding to an advertised job opening, say so in your opening paragraph. Note where you saw the ad and the date of the publication.
3. Summarize in a way that is tailored to the probable interest of this particular employer. You can preview your resume here, giving excerpts of your experience and abilities as they relate to the needs of this employer.
4. If you are self-employed, this is the proper place to insert this information and explain why you are looking for another job. If you are currently employed by a company, describe the job and tell why you are looking for a new job.
5. Here's the first punch of a one-two knockout close for your letter. Be direct. Say you want to work for the company. And give a logical reason why you'd be a good hire.
6. The action close. Say what you want, and request some specific action.

A sample introductory letter to a CEO appears on page 93. A similar letter, based on your own research of a company, could help you start networking right at the top. Even a small item in the morning newspaper or in a magazine can give you a reason to write to company executives.

PAUL B. DOE
116 N. Main Street
Moorland, CA 63185
Home phone 805/229-8700
Fax 805/229-8709

(Date)

Ms. Jenny Fairfax
Marketing Manager
Instruments, Inc.
1100 Valley View Drive
Cleveland, OH 44000-1234

Dear Ms. Fairfax:

Congratulations on moving your firm into the "top ten" new companies in this area. With the explosive growth your company has experienced in the last six months, you may well need additional help in your sales department. I would like to offer that help. I am a veteran wholesale sales manager. I can help you manage your increased sales efficiently and open new markets. My resume is enclosed.

These aspects of my background fit hand in glove with what I have learned of your company:
• I have managed sales organizations structured by regions and states.
• I have hands-on knowledge of all aspects of working with wholesalers and independent sales reps.
• I have a track record of setting ambitious but realistic sales goals and achieving or surpassing them in every one of the past six years.
• In addition, I have traveled widely through most of the Northeast and North Central Midwest regions, which seem to be your major markets.

Currently I am working as a sales promotion consultant for several companies in Ohio. However, the ups and downs of working as an independent consultant are not as satisfying as I had hoped. I want to join a growing company where I can make a major contribution in a stable environment. Previously I was a regional sales manager for Schulte Tool and Die, Inc., in Moorland, Ohio. I directed a sales force of 22, which consistently produced over 70 percent of the company's annual gross sales volume.

I am very interested in Instruments, Inc., especially because of the way you prepare your new product launches with careful marketing research. I would appreciate the opportunity of talking with you. I will call you within the next three days.

Cordially,

Paul B. Doe

IRENE CARTER
117 N. Woodson
Miami, FL 33180
Phone 305-795-4112
Fax 305-785-4335

(Date)

Mr. Charles Evans
President and CEO
Walkers Labels
Suite 15, 110 N. Halson
Miami, FL 33180

Dear Mr. Evans:

Business Week magazine recently reported that 56% of your growth had come from increased sales of new label products to South American companies. But in your *BW* interview you mentioned the problems your company was experiencing with dated equipment. I would like to know more about your company and your equipment problems. I believe I could help because of my past successful experience in solving similar problems with a Total Quality Management program I developed for two major corporations. Here are examples of just two of the actions I took in the area of TQM for Goodmonth Tire & Rubber Company:

• Organized a workers' quality circle that uncovered a new way to combine two milling operations on one machine. Warren Cross, Director of Manufacturing, said, "This action reduced our production costs 20% in just three months."

• Developed a TQM manual for upper management. The president of the company, Charles Ritsen, said, "Ms. Carter recognized early on that W. Edwards Deming's quality control concepts must be supported by upper management. Her manual was a model of clarity and good sense."

Now I would like to do the same for your organization. I realize that a position may not be available right now, but I really believe a face-to-face discussion could be of mutual value. Or you may want to refer me to another member of your organization with direct responsibilities in quality control.

I will call you next Monday to see if you might be free for a meeting during the week. I would also appreciate your secretary sending me a copy of your annual report. The *Business Week* article certainly whetted my appetite to know more!

Cordially,

Irene Carter

Interview Techniques to Close the Sale

> • *The majority of your job hunting is devoted to the goal of getting interviews with hiring authorities.*
> • *Practice, practice, practice until you are perfect.*

The interview is the crucial step between a contact and a job. But getting the interview appointment is only the start. You must then win the interview. That takes preparation. Please don't short-change this preparation, no matter how adept you believe you are at presentations or meetings. This will be a different kind of meeting.

As a result of the employer research we've urged you to complete, you will have acquired names of managers who are hiring authorities in companies you want to target for jobs. As you contact these managers, try to set up an interview. There are two kinds, both of which are valuable and can lead to new position offers—the information interview and the job interview.

INFORMATION INTERVIEWS

As the name implies, these interviews provide you with the opportunity to get information about a targeted company that will give you an advantage in securing a job with the firm. Often getting a face-to-face information interview is easier than lining up a designated job interview. Indeed, an information interview can result from a totally cold call to an employer.

With a good start on your list of researched companies, you are ready to begin calling some key executives. What you want from them is an interview. Unfortunately, a straightforward request is not always the shortest distance between what you desire and what you achieve.

For example, you call the manager. "I'd like to come in and talk to you about the job possibilities at Bigtime Industries. What is a convenient time?"

Like all managers, this one is very busy; in fact, he is harried, just keeping up with the work load. And the word is out in the company—no new hires. The manager is polite, but not at all encouraging. "I appreciate your call, but there are absolutely no openings here at this time. In fact, there is a hiring freeze in place. Sorry."

What's your comeback? "Please. I just want to get my foot in the door. Won't you give me a few minutes to talk about jobs there anyway?" That approach won't be very effective, given the candor with which the manager answered your original query.

So what then?

Back up. Remember what we said about giving yourself a creative edge? Start by going after an informational interview. You're not looking for a job, you're looking for information.

Now when you call that harried manager who has no job to offer, after identifying yourself you say, "I'd like to ask a favor of you. I'm in the midst of a major career change, and I need some advice from an expert like you. I'm thinking of starting a business in (name the field) and I want to question as many top people in the industry as I can. If you'll give me 15 minutes of your time, I'd like to come by and show you some of the products (or services) I've come up with and get your reactions. Would this be possible?"

Again developing a creative edge for yourself, you could explain that you have done a marketing study, for instance, or produced a prototype marketing newsletter that you'd like to go over with the interviewer. Thus the interviewer anticipates getting something more out of the deal than just meeting you. Your study or newsletter might well be something the interviewer's company could use.

Asking for an informational interview is a reasonable request. You have not mentioned anything about wanting a job. The manager is not threatened with the possibility of being put on the spot or having to explain why there are no jobs. In fact, you just might show the manager ideas that could make his or her job easier, or make up for the lack of manpower in the office.

If you are able to say that you got the manager's name from a mutual friend, or that you notice that he had just won an award or got a promotion, or simply that you had heard that she was something of an authority in the field, the manager probably will be all the more disposed to give you an audience.

Don't be discouraged if you get turned down on your request. You may have to make a dozen or more calls to get your first interview. Stay with it. If you have friends who can refer you to such people, use those contacts; they'll better your chances. At the behest of friends and relatives, we've all called or written to other friends and associates in business to ask them to see someone.

The person you call is likely to be flattered by your interest, especially if it is clear that you appear knowledgeable about your field (because you have collected valuable data in the course of your research and on all those Job Prospect Cards you've completed). Having gotten an appointment for an interview with your over-the-transom move, prepare to make the most of the precious 15 minutes. Stay strictly within the bounds of the time you asked for—unless the person who is hosting you asks you to stay longer, which, of course, is a very good sign that this effort is working beyond your expectations.

In your allotted time, keep your questions and comments fairly direct and straightforward—you want to learn as much as you can about the manager and his firm. At the end of the interview, ask for names of other people in the field whom you could contact for information, either in his or her company or at other firms. Now your next call for an interview will be further enhanced when you say that this manager suggested you call. If the manager you interviewed with is even halfway impressed with you and your pitch, he or she might well introduce you to an associate in the company and walk you down the hall to meet your next interview subject.

At best, at the end of your 15-minute (or longer) interview, the person you've been meeting with could offer you a job or invite you back for an official job interview. (Really—it happens!) At worst, you'll know a little more for your next interview and possible follow-up job search at this company.

Once in the manager's office, it will help to be able to deliver something of value—that report you have done on the field, or an outline of products or services you propose to build a business around.

During the course of your presentation and the ensuing conversation, you should ask as many questions about the manager's business as you can—to learn about the situation and where you might fit in, now or in the future. You shouldn't break the spell by being so crass as to ask for a job. But you must be prepared to play that card if you are dealt it. For instance, what if the manager says something like, "You know, if your business fails, you ought to apply for a job here. You'd make a good widgeteer." You could respond, "Well, that sounds more secure than my business plan. You don't have such a position open now, do you?" But in most instances, you won't be so lucky, so you'll have to leave with only the information you gleaned. But you will have left an impression on the manager that could lead to further developments. That would not have been possible had you not succeeded in getting in the door through the device of the informational interview!

In job hunting, you build on your experiences. Your fourth or fifth interview is bound to be better than your first. You'll develop a style, a pattern, and an ease of presentation that will not only impress your interviewer, but will also make you more comfortable in interviewing situations. (That's why you should *never* turn down a chance for a job interview, even when you may feel you're not fully qualified for the job. Some of our colleagues have gone to interviews for "practice" and been hired!)

The Official Job Interview

This is the one you are invited to; you can't expect to wheedle your way into this kind of meeting. The agenda is clear for this interview—it's about a job. An official job interview can be more stressful than the informational interview, because now you anticipate a make-or-break outcome.

Interviews are the doorways to jobs. Virtually no one (with the possible exception of the boss's son or daughter) can land a job without an interview. You can look great on paper. Your references can give you great support. But the person who does the hiring will want to see you, to talk with you face to face, before making a decision about offering you a job.

Bob Snelling, CEO of an employment service chain, says *people hire people.* They don't hire resumes or college credentials. They hire people they like.

So when the call comes for you to come in for an interview, treat this as you would an appearance on "Oprah" or "Donahue" or Jay Leno's "Tonight Show" or CNN's "Money Talk" or a state dinner at the White House.

Prepare for your appearance and make sure you look great when you go.

Preparation

Here's where your work with the Job Prospect Cards also pays off. Use the cards you compiled on the company you'll be interviewing with to put together a briefing paper—a profile of the company that will give you some pertinent things to ask about in the interview and that may give you some clues as to what to expect of your interviewers.

When you go to the interview, wear a freshly pressed suit or dress. Yes, that sounds trite, maybe a bit old-fashioned, and perhaps needless to say. But you'd be surprised how many job hunters make mistakes like showing up for an interview with a stained tie, a torn blouse, etc. You should be glad for these blunders made by others; they make your chances of getting the job better.

We shouldn't have to pump you up into a winning frame of mind for your job interviews. You know your capabilities, your strengths, the added value you can bring to the equation. Suffice it to say: Go to the meeting with the feeling *"I am going to get this job."*

You will want to arrive for your interview fresh, not frazzled—feeling good about your qualifications and knowledgeable about the job, the company, and the industry. It may be tough not to be nervous, but you must play this one as the professional that you are. This is not the first time you've gone one on one in a business meeting. So settle down. Be cool. And, above all, arrive on time. Get precise directions and plan for unforseen hold-ups so you can arrive early, even if you have to kill time in a coffee shop across the street. If it's a large company scattered among several adjoining buildings, find out beforehand exactly where your interviewer is located.

When you meet your interviewer, be friendly, firm, direct: "Hi, I'm Paul Doe. Nice to meet you." Once seated, the beginning of the conversation can sometimes be a bit awkward for both sides. If you sense this, signal that you are comfortable and ready to talk by bringing up a neutral subject. For example, compliment the interviewer about something in his office—a trophy, an interesting picture—and ask about it. If your research has turned up some facts such as the company's sponsorship of a golf tournament or participation in a local charity, you might talk briefly about one of these subjects. Rapport begins when you show real interest in the other person.

As the interview proceeds, look for other personal subtleties—the interviewer's body language, speech patterns, or facial expressions. Perhaps you can take advantage of this knowledge in the way you handle your end of the conversation.

Practice interviewing can be a good idea, especially if you haven't been in this kind of situation in a while. Get a friend or business associate to run you through a mock interview. You'll quickly pick up on little things you should and shouldn't do. For example, don't stare at the wall. Maintain eye contact with the interviewer. Stay interested in everything he or she is saying.

Visit several employment agencies or personnel consultants to inquire about how the firm can aid you in your search. In the process, a consultant will interview you much as an employer would. In many cases, personal consultant firms are used by employers to screen all applicants for a particular job, referring the best 10 or so to the employer for a final round of interviews.

Another way to prep for a job interview is to think of several examples of how you bring added value to a company—then be determined to work these into the conversation. Also, review questions that are most apt to be asked by employers, so that you are prepared to answer without hesitation in the actual interview. Here are some standard interview questions you may encounter:

- How would you describe yourself?
- How do you define success?
- Would you rather do a job, design the job, evaluate it, or manage others who are doing it?
- What is your greatest weakness? Your greatest strength?
- Why do you think you'd like working for this company?
- Are you creative? Give an example.
- Are you analytical? Give an example.
- You may also be asked: How do you like working for your present company (or boss)? That question may be followed by: Why do you want to leave the company?

Really listen to every question. A common mistake, usually caused by nerves, is starting to answer a question before the interviewer has finished asking it. Take a few seconds at the end of each question to gather your thoughts. Don't try to lead the interview or become a motor mouth. Interviewers want to feel that they are in charge of the meeting.

Prepare reasonable and diplomatic answers to these questions. Above all, don't bad-mouth your previous employers. You may hate them for how they treated you or for knocking you out of a job, but hold your tongue. If you rag on another employer, it's a sign your emotions have gotten the best of your judgment. It's an interview killer. A job interview should always be positive, unless you're looking for a new job because your previous company or division has gone out of business. Revealing news that has been widely reported by the press should not be detrimental for you. Unfortunate situations befall any and all of us at one time or another—they shouldn't cast doubt on a person's qualifications.

Ask questions about the company. Even if you've done some

good research on the firm, there is a lot you need to know to maneuver toward a job. Avoid naive questions such as, "How long have you been in business?" and "What products do you make?" The interviewer will expect you to know such elementary information if you were interested enough to apply for a job.

Here are some good questions to ask. The interviewer's answers could help you sharpen your own responses during the rest of the interview and any subsequent interviews for this same position.

• I've read, of course, the description of this position in your ad. Could you tell me more about any other responsibilities of the job that weren't listed?
• Where do you feel this position could lead for the right person?
• To whom would I report? Could you tell me more about what he (or she) expects of the person filling this position?

And, finally, one question that disarms many interviewers and can lead to an interesting discussion:

• Is there any question about the company or this position that *you* would have asked if you were on my side of the desk?

As YOU GO through the interview process, you may want to change your basic resume based on what you learn about the job requirements. For example, if the first interviewer says to you, "Could you come in later this week to meet Mr. Snelling?" the interviewer is obviously going to recommend that the company take a closer look at you. Ask the interviewer for a further description of the position and if you should add any relevant experience to your resume before you see Mr. Snelling. The interviewer has in effect become your partner. He or she can help you prepare for the next person you see.

Don't hesitate to get a little personal in the interview. If you think of an anecdote that would reveal how you deal with certain situations or what kind of person you are, or that will simply create a lighter moment in an otherwise serious meeting, tell it. It will show that you can relax, even in this stressful situation. At the end of the interview, don't be afraid to ask the interviewer for a candid analysis of how the interview went— something like this: "May I ask how you think this session has gone? Is there anything more you need to know about me?" If the interviewer realizes you are sincere, you could get some valuable insights or advice even if you don't get a sense of how likely you are to get this particular job. If the interviewer doesn't indicate where you stand or what the company's time frame is for reaching a decision, you should ask when you will know the outcome of your interview.

If you are told at the conclusion of the interview that you aren't the person the company is looking for, don't just slump off, dejected. Use the opportunity to ask if the interviewer could refer you to other companies where your background might be more valuable.

Afterward

Always follow up an interview with a short note thanking the interviewer for his or her time and for the opportunity to try for the job. If you are like most people, you probably will think of some things you wished you had brought up in the interview but didn't. Use your thank-you note to correct this oversight.

Here's a sample follow-up note:

Dear Ms. (or Mr.)_____:

Thanks for interviewing me for the _____ position last (day of week).

I came away from our discussion very enthusiastic about the job and your company. You did, however, raise one point in the interview that I feel I should answer more completely. You said that one of the responsibilities of the job involved setting up training classes. I neglected to mention that I was a seminar leader at two separate classes held annually by my former company. We "graduated" over twenty employees from these classes, five of whom went on to supervisory positions within five months.

If there is any additional information you need from me, please let me know. I hope to hear from you soon.

With best regards,

It's important to make notes immediately after every interview. File them with your cover letter and other research material you've collected on the company. This will prove valuable if you are called back for additional interviews with the firm. Often on the way to getting a job offer, you may have interviews with two, three, or more executives in the company. The higher the position you are seeking, the more people you're likely to have to talk to at the company. By reviewing your notes of each session you can be sure to include questions you have about the company, avoid areas that appear to be sensitive, and expand on points you made in earlier meetings. If you are called back for additional interviews, the first person who saw you obviously recommended you. Call this first interviewer for a more complete description of the job, and ask for suggestions in preparing for the second interview. This person *wants* you to look good in additional interviews since you were his or her choice for the final cut.

If you don't get any response after the interview, don't hesitate to call several days later. The person who interviewed you will feel some obligation to give you a report on what has been happening to your application. If you don't get through directly to the person you are calling, don't leave a message for your call to be returned. Don't even leave your name. Simply say that you will call again. This gives you the freedom to call several times without prejudicing the secretary against you.

The Stress Interview

You may never encounter it, but you should be prepared for the so-called stress interview. It is characterized by a series of tough, pointed questions designed to put you on the spot to come up with reasonable replies. Some of the questions will strike you as too personal. Perhaps their point is to challenge you to decide quickly whether to answer or instead to suggest that the question is out of line.

Interviewers ask these kinds of questions to pierce the veil of a candidate who has carefully prepared answers to standard interview questions. The interviewer wants to see how the individual will respond without a mental "script," just as that person would to a real-life job situation.

Stress interviewers aren't interested in whether your answers are "right" or "wrong"—they want to know how you react under pressure. It's really your composure that's being put to the test. Here's a sampling:

- *What can you do for us that someone else can't?*
- *What salary are you worth?*
- *What makes you angry?*
- *Why haven't you obtained a new job so far?*
- *Tell me about situations in which your work was criticized.*
- *What interests you least about this job?*
- *Don't you feel you might be better off in a different type of company?*
- *Why aren't you earning more money?*
- *How is your family life?*
- *How is your health?*
- *Were you fired from your last position?*
- *What do your subordinates think of you?*
- *Will you be out to take your boss's job?*

Simply knowing that these kinds of questions may be asked will diminish their shock value. If you anticipate questions like these and prepare some good solid comebacks (responses that are as neutral as possible) that you can deliver in a calm, unrattled voice, you will have passed the test. The interviewer might even end this line of questioning, if you're handling the situation with aplomb.

Here are some examples of possible responses to tough questions:

What makes you angry?

People who don't pull their weight on a team project.

What interests you least about this job?

So far I haven't discovered any negatives about it. I'll be asking you some questions as we go along if I see any.

Will you go after the boss's job in several months?

I'll be out to support my boss in every way I can. At the same time I hope I can learn everything about my boss's job, so that I can move into that spot when he or she moves up, thanks to my help.

See how disarming these answers are? You can pull it off if you are confident and relaxed going into any interview. Remember that even in a stress interview there are some questions a prospective employer can't ask you. For example, current fair-employment practices prohibit questions about your age, whether you are divorced, etc. If asked, you can politely decline to answer.

For a comprehensive rundown of stress questions and possible answers, see *How to Turn an Interview into a Job*, by Jeffrey G. Allen (A Fireside Book, Simon & Schuster).

Job Interview Killers

- *Smoking or chewing gum*
- *Addressing the interviewer by first name*
- *Not listening and constantly interrupting the interviewer*
- *Not answering the questions asked*
- *Looking at your watch*
- *Avoiding eye contact by looking out the window during the conversation*

"When interviewing I look for a balance between a person's ability to work effectively on a team and also to take on responsibilities and work independently when necessary. My second most important criterion is the person's ability to keep going at a moving target, to cope in a constantly changing environment."
Roger Knight
Marketing Manager, K-12 Education Division
Apple Computer, Inc.

Rehearse, Rehearse, Rehearse

Whenever you're invited to an interview, jump at the chance (even if you feel you are over- or underqualified). Each interview gives you an opportunity to improve your interviewing techniques and to become more at ease handling even the toughest questions.

Ask several business friends to conduct mock interviews with you. Dress just as you would for a regular interview, and bring your resume and any presentation material with you. If possible, record these interviews with a tape recorder or camcorder. The playback can help you improve immeasurably.

Have your friends ask the same kind of questions they might use in interviewing someone for their firms. Tell them not to hold off asking tough, surprise questions to try to throw you off balance. Then ask them to be totally candid in rating you using this scorecard. (Many hiring authorities today rate you based on the categories shown on this card.)

INTERVIEW RATING CARD

Rating scale 1-10 (1 = unacceptable, 10 = excellent)

Work Experience   _____

Knowledge of Job   _____

Communication Skills   _____

Creativity   _____

Motivation   _____

Initiative   _____

Appearance   _____

Composure   _____

Attitude   _____

Overall Rating   _____

Should We Hire This Person? ( ) Yes ( ) No

FOURTEEN

Computerizing Your Search

> • *Set up a computer to handle your correspondence and much of your research.*
> • *(Or) find a computer buff who will do this for you.*

Andrew Grove, the CEO of Intel, was quoted in *Fortune* magazine as saying, "In all business, to provide value, you've got to do whatever it is you do fast and with immense efficiency. Why do you think everybody is buying computers?"

Why not apply the awesome power of the computer to speeding your search for a job? As we've stressed throughout this program, the more hiring authorities you can reach with targeted communications, the faster you can return to full employment. The computer can help you reach this goal at megahertz speed.

Even if you feel you are not computer-literate or if you don't have access to a personal computer, please read this chapter anyway. At the end of this section we'll suggest ways you can tap some awesome computer power in your job search, even if "DOS," "hard disk," and "download" are all Greek to you.

Here are six ways you can use a computer in your job search.

1. Record, collect, and organize all of the data in this 30-day program—including your Job Prospect Cards, Life Experience Cards, and company research.

2. Create your own distinctive letterhead, business cards, and self-marketing brochures with simple, new desktop publishing programs.
3. Prepare customized correspondence and resumes in minutes, directly targeted at specific jobs and companies.
4. Correspond with prospective employers instantly by E-mail and fax.
5. Use on-line data bases to research your hottest Job Prospects, check recruitment ads, and network with people in your field around the country.
6. Use new telephone-contact software to reach up to 50 to 60 people a day to get information about companies, acquire new networking names, and set up interviews.

Organize Your Data

You can begin to use the computer from the first day of your job search by setting up your own data base. This simply means using one of the data management software programs to create your own computerized card file. Most programs operate in the same way. First you type the labels you see on your Life Experience and Job Prospect Cards (such as company name, address, etc.). These labels appear on the screen each time you call up that particular file. You then add the information that changes from card to card.

Every time you get another name of an executive at a certain company or acquire a new fact from your research, you can add that information to the computer card you've already set up for that organization. You can also create a separate card for each of your networking contacts.

Once you've completed a series of cards, you can organize and manipulate them. For example, you might group together cards about those companies you consider your best prospects. You could also group Life Experience Cards under different broad headings such as "People Skills," "Technical Skills," etc. Then when you print them as a group, you can easily match them with the job requirements stated in a recruitment ad and prepare your cover letter and resume.

Even after you've found your job, it's a good idea to continue to update these files. They become a ready-to-use support system for any future job searches or career-building moves.

CREATE YOUR OWN STATIONERY

Even if your training in art ended with finger painting in the third grade, a computer can help you prepare distinctive letterhead, business cards, and resume "brochures." Today relatively inexpensive desktop publishing programs provide templates for your stationery and other literature. You just replace the type you see on the screen with your own words and drop in clip art from other computer disks. You are also free to change the size and font of the type to suit your preference. (See the example of a computer-generated letterhead on page 110. Distinctive business card and resume brochure formats are presented in the next chapter.)

CUSTOMIZE YOUR LETTERS AND RESUMES

Once you've created a basic introductory letter to a CEO, or a cover letter, or a resume, you can use a computer to tailor them specifically to certain companies and job openings. The secret is in the use of boilerplate text, a technique used by many direct-mail companies to personalize letters or change the terms of an offer. For example, each of your Life Experience Cards ends with a resume bullet—a factual summary of that experience that you can use in your cover letter or resume. You could store all of these bullet sentences in a computer file, each with a different number. Print pages that summarize all of these bullets.

Now you can "copy" and "paste" these paragraphs into your correspondence to match the needs of a particular company, as stated in a help-wanted ad or job description. Or, if you're working with someone who is supplying you with computer services, you can mark your cover letter with a note indicating the changes you want in this basic document that is stored in the computer: "Add paragraphs 1, 7, and 19." You can do the same with a resume.

This allows you to do your basic correspondence "by the numbers" and save a tremendous amount of time. You still have

John L. Meister
Accountant

12 E. 85th St. New York, NY 10158   212-879-5666
FAX 212-879-5900

An example of computer-generated stationery

the flexibility to add individual items you've discovered in your research to update your applications.

Software can help you create individual resumes tailored to a particular job. PFS: Resume and Job Search Pro, by Spinnaker, is one of the best sellers in this category. This program lets you choose from nine different resume styles, from a fast "no-frills" version to specialized resume versions for "Engineer," "Professional," and "Academic" applications. The computer asks you questions about your background and you type the answers. The program then organizes your background under appropriate headings, checks all the spelling, and arranges the information according to the resume style you've selected. Your document is then ready to be printed and mailed. PFS: Resume and Job Search Pro offers other useful features, such as a thesaurus that helps you replace dull, plodding words with action-oriented verbs that make your resume (and you) sound more dynamic. You can use the program's word processor to prepare cover letters, and use its contact and calendar features to record the names of every hiring authority you call or write and to note the dates for interviews or follow-up calls.

Everyone who has applied for a government job knows about the four-page Form SF-171 that must be submitted with each application. Because most of the information remains the same with only minor readjustments, the computer is a natural for completing endless versions of this form for you, with software known as "Quick and Easy 171s" from Data Tech Distributors, Inc., of Harrisburg, PA.

INSTANT CORRESPONDENCE

Would you like to survey 50 companies about their hiring needs for the next four weeks? Would this afternoon be soon enough? Using electronic mail and on-line data bases and communication companies, you can write a basic survey letter, then prepare a list of the 50 companies with addresses. With a few keystrokes you can instantly transmit that letter electronically to the companies (if they have an "electronic mailbox") or by hard copy to be delivered by the U.S. Post Office one to two days later. (This feature alone saves you hours or even days of time that you would otherwise spend writing, addressing, and mailing your letters.) Want to send the same survey letter to another 50 companies? Just tell the computer to send letter A to list B, which is comprised of the new names and addresses you've added. You can also use the computer to send and receive faxes. If you have several standard resumes on file in your computer, you could send your application to a company within seconds of a request. The fax is a very effective communications medium because of the sense of urgency it conveys.

INSTANT RESEARCH AND NETWORKING

On-line data bases such as Compuserv (the largest), Prodigy, GEnie, America Online, and Delphi can accelerate your job search with a wide variety of services:

Research

You can review (and print) recent magazine and newspaper articles about your job prospects. Compuserv lets you set up a "personal folder" that automatically collects and stores every published news item or article about a company or industry you've selected. Set up a personal folder for each of your five best job prospects and another for your industry specialty. The data base will then scan magazines, articles, and newsletters for information about the topics you've selected. This feature alone can save a number of trips to the library and can often provide you with dozens of names of hiring authorities within a company. You can also check stock prices and stock evaluations of all public companies, which translate into good tips on new product introductions and expansions that could forecast hiring activity.

Review Help-Wanted Ads

Many of the data bases carry recruitment ads from all over the country, often with a much more comprehensive description of the job requirements than you would find in typical newspaper ads. You can respond with your cover letter and resume electronically—and instantly.

Electronic Networking

You can reach people all over the country. The computer on-line services offer a variety of professional "forums" that help people with similar interests meet and "talk" via the computer. We've participated in these professional forums for a number of months and find that many professionals really try to help each other with information, answers to questions about particular industries, and candid discussions of mutual problems. This is the essence of networking in its most efficient form, and it can lead to new friendships and job leads.

Many of the on-line services are now paying more attention

to the needs of job hunters. For example, Online America has established "The Career Center." Subscribers can browse through resume and cover letter templates that can be downloaded to a job hunter's computer. If you subscribe to the service, you could schedule a private session (on screen) with a job counselor, complete an aptitude test and interest exercises to help you determine new career directions, and even list your qualifications in the center's talent data base, which can be viewed by companies looking for new employees.

One caution. While these on-line services can save you hours of research time, they can also become very expensive if you stay connected for too long or use their "extended" services (translation: extra fees) too frequently. You can reduce costs by shopping around (recently these on-line data bases have been sniping each other in a continuing price war) and by knowing exactly what information you're looking for even before you turn the computer on. Some public libraries (for a modest fee or even for free) will let you use their computers to get information from on-line data bases.

We suggest getting the basic literature of each of the on-line services and comparing costs before you make your decision. Here are their toll-free numbers.

America Online	800-827-6364
Compuserv	800-848-8199
Delphi	800-695-4005
GEnie	800-638-9636
Prodigy	800-776-3449

AUTOMATED PHONE AND MAIL

We recently asked a top salesman how he was able to talk with dozens of people every day and then fax or mail them reports and letters before he quit at 5 P.M. His secret: contact software.

He uses this software to record the basic information for each of his current customers and his best prospects: name, title, company name, address, phone, etc. His computer is connected to the phone system with a modem. He can call each of the individuals by using a computer mouse to point at an icon of a telephone on the screen. If he arranges a meeting or interview during the call, he records this information in special spaces on a contact record that fills the screen. After the call, he points the mouse at another icon with a pencil—the symbol for correspondence. Instantly the basic format of a letter appears on the screen with all of the basic information already complete: the prospect's name, title, company, and address, then the salutation and a "sincerely yours" close, followed by the salesman's name and the current date.

He types his message and then can send it by fax or electronic mail so that it arrives on the individual's desk within the next few seconds. Or he can have the letter printed, along with an envelope.

The software also maintains a history of every phone call or letter he has written to that individual, along with other information—agreements reached, future meetings or phone calls to be scheduled, and incidental information picked up during the call about that person, his or her company, and the industry in general. It's no wonder that this salesman can call or write 40 to 50 people per day and that his monthly sales are light-years ahead of his colleagues.

The software we have described in this example is Act for Windows. Other contact software is widely available. You can purchase mailing lists on disk that you can merge with your contact software. Just one example: Demand Research in Chicago sells computer disks with lists of up to 600 job prospects in your field. When you merge this with your contact software, you instantly have access to the company names, address, and phone numbers, and the names of the CEO and the CFO (chief financial officer). This same information, if compiled from directories in the library, could require hours of work. Call Demand Research at 312-664-6500 for current prices and more information. Unlike most other mailing lists, you can make unlimited phone and mail use of their names.

If You Don't Have a Computer

Anyone who can type or two-finger a keyboard can learn to operate a computer. The software has now become so simple that you can do much of the work by touching one key or by maneuvering a "mouse" across a flat surface to control an on-screen pointer.

If you don't have one now, you probably don't want to plunk down $3,000 to $4,000 for a computer and laser printer. But there are alternatives. The price of used computers is dropping rapidly. You can often find good buys in the classified ads. You may also want to consider renting a computer and printer during your job search, or borrowing these machines from a relative. Software is expensive, but there are numerous low-cost alternatives such as Freeware and Shareware. Some computer programmers have created new word processing, spread sheet, and publishing software that they offer free of charge—or at a very low price—to computer owners. Their pitch: If you like the program, you then send them a small amount of money and receive complete documentation and updates on the program, which is a very good deal. Some of the on-line data bases also let subscribers download software to their own computers.

There's even a bonus to becoming more computer literate: You become a more marketable job candidate. Companies are always looking for people with computer skills.

IF YOU HATE COMPUTERS

You still don't have to give up the awesome job-getting potential of a computer. Consider hiring a high school or college student who has the equipment and the skills. For many students today, computers are a second language.

Or look for a fellow job hunter who is also knowledgeable about computers. You could divide up projects, with your computer buff associate writing and printing correspondence and you manning the phone. You could find such people at local job-getting clubs or place an ad in the local paper.

This is a flat-out prediction: A computer with the right software can at least double the number of people you can comfortably contact each day. And that's the name of the job-hunting game.

Sharpening Your

Creative Edge

> • *Separate yourself from the crowd of other applicants by demonstrating new ideas in your job search.*

"Promise, large promise, is the soul of an advertisement," Dr. Samuel Johnson said in the 18th century. He demonstrated this when he created a notice for an auction of the contents of a London brewery. "We are not here to sell boilers and vats but the potential of growing rich beyond the dreams of avarice."

Dr. Johnson was among the early practitioners of the art of separating himself from the crowd by giving himself a creative edge.

In the first part of this book we've stressed the importance of applying the traditional job-getting techniques (networking, responding to help-wanted ads, and working with employment agencies) in a highly structured way. That's because these tried-and-true techniques have helped millions of people find profitable employment over the past several decades.

But you are also aware that something new and troubling is happening in today's job market. Whole floors and buildings have been emptied of mid-level executives and professionals who have often been forced onto the street with little or no notice. Because many have been unable to find similar positions with the same levels of perks, authority, and compensation, they have started to hunt for jobs lower down the ladder. This has sharply increased both the number and quality of people competing for the same jobs. The displacement wave has extended all the way down the corporate "food chain," forcing recent college grads to compete with former executives of companies such as IBM and Sears for positions at the same salary level. More often than not, companies select veterans with proven track records and "bargain" price tags. College grads in turn displace high school grads in flipping burgers and doing clerical work.

This intensified competition is showing up constantly in the large number of resumes sent by highly qualified people, and by the growing lines of people at job fairs and in front of every company that places recruitment ads in the Sunday papers.

What does all this mean to you in terms of your personal job search? You still must write "killer" cover letters and resumes and develop presentation skills. During the go-go '80s, such talents would have probably landed you a good job in a matter of days or even hours. Today they are often just the price of admission to the final cut of a company's job search.

For example, Merck receives 200,000 resumes annually for positions at all levels (or an average of 770 every working day). AT&T's mailbag bulges with 100,000 annually (an average of 385 every day).

Here's a hypothetical example of what those numbers might mean to you if you were applying for a position at Merck. You might assume that perhaps only a scant 3 percent of all applicants had the qualifications for or interest in that particular job. Furthermore, you might also assume that only about 10 percent of those would have really outstanding credentials or work experience. *That still leaves 600 top-level candidates for the position you want!*

How can you compete against this rising tide?

Continue to use the traditional job-getting techniques. They can still get you in the door. If you're one of a limited number of competitors for an availability you've discovered in the hidden job market, these techniques could get you the job.

But if you find these techniques are not generating the kind of response you want from employers, try giving yourself a creative edge that separates you from your competition. Fortunately there is a whole warehouse of ideas and efficient tools from other fields—such as journalism, marketing, and others—that are underused or never used in job hunting.

By urging you to become more creative in your job search, we are not talking about doing "wild and crazy" things to call attention to yourself, such as sending resumes on colored paper in a pizza box or appearing in clown makeup at trade shows (unless, of course, it's a convocation of clowns). Indeed, sometimes the unconventional works simply because it attracts attention in a new and different way. A number of Washington University (St. Louis) college students posed for pictures in baseball uniforms and created baseball cards with their photos and "stats" (quick summaries of their school and work experiences). Many of them got jobs. A man seeking a marketing assignment from a pet food manufacturer took his dog to the interview. He got the assignment because the company interviewers were so impressed by his empathy with their ultimate customers.

But these are exceptions—most American businesspeople are inherently conservative. If your resume in menu format does arrive in a pizza box, company execs may be more bemused than impressed. Instead we urge you use relational creativity—that is, finding new ways to demonstrate your ability to do the job and bring added value to their companies. For example, in this chapter we will show you a new kind of resume that uses computer graphics that visually summarize your experience. It gives the resume reader an instant snapshot of your career to date in a chart format that is familiar to everyone.

Here are some other ways you can give yourself a creative edge through relational creativity. *Remember: Use your imagination to beat your competition.*

•*Benchmark your job application.* Benchmarking is a new buzz word in American industry. It means keeping an eye on your competition and incorporating their best ideas into your "product"—in this case, your presentation. Most job hunters operate in a vacuum. But you should take every opportunity to see what cover letters and resumes are getting attention. If you have friends or former co-workers who recently got jobs, ask them to explain how they did it and ask for copies of their resumes. Review some of the excellent books in the library that are compilations of successful resumes and cover letters. These include *Resumes That Knock 'em Dead* and *Cover Letters that Knock 'em Dead,* both by Martin Yate. Your reference librarian can suggest others. Use all this information to make your application as good as—*or better*—than your competition.

•*Respond instantly.* A basic problem many execs face today is getting their staff to do things on time. Any applicant who shows a clear understanding of the value of time can move ahead of the others—quickly. For example, in an interview you've just completed, the company's human resources director requests some additional information about the part you personally played in the development of a new product at your previous company. You discuss this with him. But after you leave the office, you slap your forehead, remembering a key point you forgot to make. If you have a laptop computer, write your more complete response in the lobby and give it to his secretary. You can also do the same thing by working with a nearby secretarial service or sending a fax. When your response and thank-you note arrive within several minutes or hours of your interview, the exec may well realize how important it would be to have someone so responsive on staff.

•*Make your cover letters stand out.* Most business correspondence is dull and lifeless, filled with standard clichés and bureaucratic jargon. That usually goes double for many of the cover letters and other letters job hunters send out. "In response to your advertisement of June 2 in the *Baltimore Sun,* I would like to send you my application for this interesting position"—the balance of the letter is equally gripping.

In advertising you learn that nine times as many people read the ad headline as read the body copy. Think of the first line of your cover letter as your headline. Does it compel the reader to read on? Keep a "swipe file" of business direct-mail letters you get from correspondence courses, seminars, encyclopedia firms, and insurance companies. These are often written by copywriters who earn up to $5,000 a letter because they know how to get a response through their words. Their techniques are easy to learn. Notice how their first sentence immediately grabs you, often with a promise of a specific benefit for you and how they build interest and use emotion and short anecdotes to keep you reading. Many use testimonials to build credibility. You can do the same in your cover letters.

A friend of ours in the travel business recently came into our office with a copy of an ad for a director of a large tour firm in the Midwest. He wanted to apply and showed us the draft of his cover letter.

You guessed it. The first line read, "In response to your advertisement of May 15, I would like to apply for the position of director of tour operations." This opening was followed by three more "standard" paragraphs about his interest in the job, his past experience, and his desire for an interview.

Our critique: "Almost everyone who applies is going to send this kind of clichéd letter. What makes your application any different?"

His face reddened and he shouted, "This is the first position I've seen advertised for which I was absolutely qualified!"

Our suggestion: "Why not use those exact words as the first line of your cover letter? Emotion and enthusiasm are catching. Companies want people who are enthusiastic about their jobs. It could be your creative edge."

•*Conduct a survey.* After you have targeted certain companies as your top job prospects, talk to some of their customers. For example, if you are applying for a manufacturing position with a company that makes garden tractors, call 10 to 15 garden and hardware stores in your area and ask them about certain brands of garden tractors. Then write a brief report on your findings. This report is catnip for almost every executive in your targeted company (as well as other organizations in the same industry). Most businesspeople love learning about their customers, even via what we call "grandmother" research—research conducted in an unscientific way. When you first write to the CEO of your target company, mention this survey and offer to bring it to his or her office. Do not enclose it. Make the executive contact you. Most CEOs will be impressed by your enterprise and will respond. This type of letter usually flies right past the gatekeepers. (Secretaries generally know what their bosses like to see.)

As a second effort (remember, make every action count twice), send your survey to the business section of the local newspaper or as a press release to trade magazines, for example, in the garden industry—with your name listed as the person conducting the survey. Most publications are very enthusiastic about virtually any survey in their field. If they print it, you will have an authoritative clipping to send out with your resume.

Following are more ways to give your application a creative edge. Your goal is simple. To make hiring authorities say to themselves *(and* their superiors), "We need this kind of problem solver."

Three Ways to Become More Creative

1. **Read widely. You can't think on an empty mind.**
2. **Don't censor your ideas. Write down everything that comes to mind about ways to separate yourself from other job seekers. One day later you can become a "critic" and prune your list.**
3. **Put your ideas into action. Otherwise your creative edge is only an empty slogan.**

THE EXPERIENCE GRAPH

Here's a new idea that can make your resume attract favorable attention in three to five *seconds!* That's the average amount of time a hiring authority spends initially reading a resume—and if the resume doesn't stand out from the crowd, there may not be a second reading.

Why not capture your future boss's attention instantly with a visual tool, an experience graph, featured right at the top of your resume. You can use computer spreadsheet software to create a chart that instantly summarizes your areas of expertise. An experience graph is attractive and comprehensive, and a prospective employer does not have to read through your whole resume to see your major strengths.

On page 123 we show how to give your credentials a new image. It's also quick and easy. Anyone with a computer and spreadsheet/graph software can create this chart in about 60 seconds. (In creating this chart we used an IBM-clone computer and a Microsoft Works software program.)

THE RESUME BROCHURE

Another way to *command* attention is to turn your resume into a brochure.

Sending a brochure with a promise on the cover is another way to distinguish yours from the crowd of resumes that are often as alike as identical peas in a pod. Cost a fortune to prepare a brochure? The one on page 125 cost about two cents worth of bond paper. All the type was set on a computer (an IBM-clone, using Microsoft Windows and Microsoft Publisher software). And you do not have to be a computer buff. You can hire a college or high school student who already has a computer (and some of these students really *are* computer geniuses).

You can produce your own personal brochure in color for less than forty cents per copy. Paper Direct preprints a variety of folder shells in attractive designs in full color. You can buy this folder paper, use Paper Direct's computer templates (which show you exactly where to type the words), and have your text laser-printed right on the folder. Some of the papers available are even scored with pop-out Rolodex cards. (You can put your name, address, and phone number on these cards; they're convenient for a personnel director who may want to reach you in the near future!) For details, call Paper Direct for a free catalog of brochures and other presentation materials at 800-272-7377.

PAUL B. DOE
116 N. Main St.
Moorland, CA 63185
Home phone 805/229-8700
Fax 805/229-8709

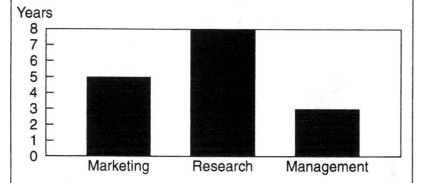

PROFESSIONAL BACKGROUND

Sales Management

Managing sales has been the major focus of my work with companies such as Playfun Games, Inc., of Los Angeles, Schulte Tool and Die of Salt Lake City, and South Coast Temps in San Diego, California. Have directed sales forces of more than 20 persons; set up training programs for regional and national sales reps. Have led sales teams to improved annual sales gains nine years in a row.

Marketing

The underlying strength of my sales management experience has been my overall marketing knowledge and skills. At Schulte Tool and Die my strategies consistently produced over 40 percent of the company's annual gross sales volume. Designed a marketing plan for South Coast Temps that produced the largest number of new client accounts in a single quarter.

Market Research

Have solid foundations in the principles and practical applications of market research. With Playfun Games, conducted market research studies which were the basis for direct-mail promotions that produced a response rate of better than 3.2 percent.

For an even more dramatic and attention-getting resume, use an experience graph as the cover sheet of your resume. The graph below was created in two minutes with Lotus Freelance Graphics software on an IBM-clone computer.

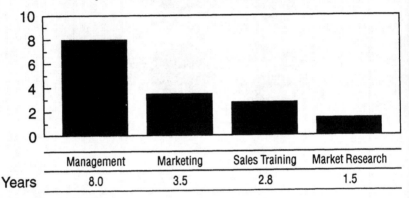

PAUL B. DOE

Experienced and successful in these areas

	Management	Marketing	Sales Training	Market Research
Years	8.0	3.5	2.8	1.5

BUSINESS CARDS AS MINI-ADS

Creative edge: See page 126 and turn your business cards into mini-ads for yourself—use the *back!* They will work twice as hard for you when you pass them out at trade shows, business meetings, job fairs, etc.

Note to computer buffs: This card was produced in about 15 minutes using a Microsoft Publish program and Lotus SmartPics for Windows. The card can also be printed from a disk in color. The help you get from computers today can help separate you from the crowd.

Paul B. Doe

Bottom-line
Marketing

> *"My fifteen years of successful sales marketing experience can help solve three of the thorniest problems facing most companies' sales departments today."*

My direct mail program sold $7 million of these toys.

Put a promise in your subhead. Companies like profit-oriented employees.

Keep reminding the company what you can do for them. But don't tell all on the cover. Make them <u>open</u> your brochure.

Put a picture of a product or service you've been involved with on the cover.

(FRONT)

John L.
Meister

912 E. 85th St., New York, NY 10158
Phone 212-879-5666 FAX 212-879-5900
(Please see back of this card.)

(BACK)

Ten years professional accounting experience.

<u>One example of assistance I can provide:</u>
Have helped over 20 companies obtain
additional bank or public financing with
comprehensive spreadsheets and reports.

Call me at 212-879-5666 for more examples
of problems I can solve for your company.

Part III

30 Days to a Good Job
Your Step-by-Step Daily Work Schedule

Jobs can be only minutes away when you target the right hiring authority. Said a former senior hiring officer at Merck, "I usually knew within three minutes after meeting a person if I was going to hire that individual. Then it was their job to lose if their interview wasn't effective or their references didn't check out."

We suggest you start your 30-day program on a Monday, the start of the work week. Weekends are ideal for research, catching up on your correspondence, and "soft" networking. For example, you could spend all day Saturday at the public library completing several dozen Job Prospect Cards. This would free you to make more "hard" networking calls at the start of the work week. You could devote Sunday to improving your resume, cover letter, and "scripts" for your networking calls. At some point during the weekend you should invite someone you care about to a movie, a museum, or a game of tennis. After all, when you're feeling the strains of the job search, so are the people who care about you.

Although many of the daily "assignments" are listed in order, you should try to do much of your research and reading (newspapers, company reports, etc.) in the evenings. This leaves you free to spend much of your day networking with hiring authorities.

This schedule is designed to keep you productive and turning up job leads throughout the day. But remember, *you* are in charge of the schedule. You can make any modifications that you feel are necessary. For example, if you get a call on Wednesday from a company that wants to interview you on Friday, set aside all of your prearranged activities and concentrate on researching that organization and preparing for that all-important interview. After you have returned from the interview, you can resume these programmed activities.

What you don't want to do is take a few days off to visit friends or go fishing. You wouldn't have done that in your previous position if you were in the midst of an important project. You shouldn't do it while working for You, Inc.

Some job hunters tell us they function more efficiently if they maintain all the routines of their previous jobs: They set the alarm, shower and shave, get dressed in suits or dresses, and "go to work." The suits and dresses may be extreme (except for interview days, of course), but sweat suits are out, too—even when you're at home.

As a professional, you should be ready to see business people throughout the day, and you should look like one. This reminds friends and co-workers that you are concentrating on business.

Now it's time to set the alarm for an early start tomorrow.

DAY ONE MONDAY

Hope you had a good night's sleep. You have a full day of work ahead of you!

- **20-Minute Wake-up Exercise.** Your choice—a brisk walk, bicycle ride, aerobics workout (if your physician agrees). Your goal is to increase your heart rate. This increases the supply of blood to the brain and can make you more productive throughout the day.

  This exercise period is a quiet time to set goals for the day ahead and to continuously critique and fine-tune your job search. For example, as you exercise today, visualize your goal: a job. What does a job provide? A chance to pay off your bills? A new car? A vacation in the year ahead? An opportunity to help your children or parents with expenses? Really *see* those things happening in your mind's eye. These can be just a few of your rewards for all your hard efforts in the next 30 days. Goals are simply *dreams with deadlines.*

- **Media Review.** Read morning newspapers, particularly the business section, so you'll be on top of what's happening in the world. Look for information about organizations that are expanding, executives who are being promoted or transferred, and companies reporting higher earnings. Almost anything that moves in the corporate world could be a job opportunity.

  Reserve some time in the evening to read trade magazines and newsletters. Mark all relevant items for clipping and filing, including appropriate help-wanted ads.

- **Research.** Complete at least five Job Prospect Cards, based on the information gleaned from your reading. Three of those cards should be for smaller companies (fewer than 100 employees). That's where the hiring action is today.

- Answer each of the help-wanted ads you've marked with a good cover letter and your resume. If you feel you are particularly qualified for certain positions, create individualized resumes that closely match your job experiences with the requirements stated in the ad.

- Visit your local library. Look for information about the five organizations you have chosen as job prospects. (If you haven't yet chosen them, use the library's resources to complete this assignment. See Chapter Seven on research for a complete list of library references to check.)

- Complete five or more Life Experience Cards. Really dig into your past. Did you learn a foreign language? Did you serve as a volunteer for a United Way campaign? Write it down. The more cards in your file, the more you can target your qualifications toward a specific job.

- **Network:** Call each of the companies listed on your Job Prospect Cards. Ask to speak to the supervisor or head of the department you would like to work for. Tell him or her of your interest in working for the company, and summarize your qualifications. If he or she is too busy to talk with you, ask if there is someone else in the company you should contact. Try to get a name and title; then call that individual. Now that you have been referred by one of their colleagues, your second call will get more attention.

- Write a letter about your job interest to the CEO of each of the five companies on your Job Prospect Cards and attach it to a resume. (See sample CEO letter in Chapter Twelve.) Use this letter to express your interest in the company and industry. If you're working with a computer or a secretarial service, use boilerplate copy to customize each of these letters and mail them today.

- Complete one or more of the Strategic Projects listed in Part Four.

- Call two or three of your former co-workers this evening. Tell them of your current job search and ask them for the names of any individuals or companies they would suggest you contact.

   Creative Edge: Talk about previous successful projects you've worked on together, and ask them what they felt your contribution to the project was. Write down their answers (if favorable), then ask if you can use their quote and name in your cover letters. These third-party endorsements are priceless and much more credible than if you presented the same information in your own words.

- Note everyone you called today in your Contact Notebook.

Group Your Projects to Save Time

You will become more efficient if you make all of your
morning or afternoon phone calls at one time. Then set
aside another period when you handle all of your correspondence for the day. At the end of the day, file all of
the information, clippings, etc., you have gathered on
specific companies in separate job folders. Now file
these away. Nothing will slow you down more the next
morning than a vertical pile of folders, notes, and
books.

Day Two Tuesday

- **20-Minute Wake-up Exercise.** Think about: What type of job do I really want? What previous jobs gave me the greatest satisfaction?
- **Media Review.** Morning newspapers. Trade magazines and newsletters. Mark all relevant items for clipping and filing, including appropriate help-wanted ads. Look for information about companies reporting higher earnings. Be sure to see the *Wall Street Journal* today; the paper's heaviest concentration of recruitment ads is on Tuesdays.
- **Research.** Complete at least five Job Prospect Cards, based on the information gleaned from your reading. Three of those cards should be for smaller companies (fewer than 100 employees).
- Complete five or more Life Experience Cards. Review some past business correspondence to remind you of past projects.
- Answer each of the help-wanted ads you've marked. Give special attention to those for which you are most qualified.
- **Network:** Call each of the companies listed on your Job Prospect Cards. Ask to speak to the supervisor or head of the department you would like to work for, and tell him or her of your interest in the field. Then make a pitch for an informational interview.
- Write a letter to the CEO of each of your five new job prospects. Do not send a resume at this time. Try a different twist. Ask for an informational interview. You want to start building his or her interest in you.
- Complete one or more of the Strategic Projects listed in Part Four.
- Tonight call at least three friends (from college, military service, etc.). After catching up on what's new, tell them you are looking for a position and would appreciate any suggestions of companies or individuals to call. Write these names in your Contact Notebook.

Before You Go to Sleep Tonight

Read the current issue of *Business Week,* the *Wall Street Journal,* and/or *Fortune* magazine. These are good sources of information about current business topics that make for effective "small talk" at the beginning of your coming interviews. Be sure to clip articles about the industries you're currently pursuing in your job hunt.

Think about the kind of work you really want to do for the rest of your life. Marcus Aurelius once said, "A man's life is what his thoughts make of it."

DAY THREE WEDNESDAY

- **20-Minute Wake-up Exercise.** Think about: What career would I like to have one year from now? Five years from now?
- **Media Review.** Scan all local newspapers. Look for news about companies already listed on your Job Prospect Cards and new companies to add to the list. Are there any stories concerning your industry? Check community calendars to find at least one meeting coming up that would be likely to attract the people you want to network with. Then call to see if you can be invited as a guest. Don't overlook the United Way, the cancer society, and other charity meetings. These often attract top business leaders. Of course, circle any help-wanted ads that sound like "you."
- **Research.** Respond to ads you've circled in your media review.
- Complete five Job Prospect Cards based on your reading and your phone conversations last night with your friends. Call the personnel departments of these companies and gather the names of hiring authorities. "Could you tell me who heads your purchasing department? Would you spell that, please?" Make every call count twice. If the company is publicly traded, ask to be switched to the investor relations department and request an annual report (often a treasure trove of information about the company and executive names).
- Complete five or more Life Experience Cards. Are you starting to run dry? Divide your recent history into three-year segments. Where were you living then? Where were you working? Does this bring back memories of special projects you had forgotten? Perhaps you helped a friend build a house. Write it down. Or set up a phone bank of volunteers for a public-TV fund-raising drive. Write it down. You've done a lot more with your life than you probably realize.
- **Network:** Write a letter to the hiring authorities you've identified at each of the five new companies you've just added to your Job Prospect Cards. Use your Life Experience Cards to add skills or experiences that might be particularly applicable to the individual companies.
- Review any responses you've received from employment agen-

cies, per the inquiries you sent out when you read Chapter Nine. Call them and ask to speak to an employment counselor. Ask about hiring activity in your specialty. Request an application if you are impressed by the counselor.

- Call each of the people recommended by your former co-workers and friends during your past two evenings of conversation. Always have two specific goals in mind for each call you make. Ask if you can come in for a short informational interview. (Do not ask for a job interview. This puts people on the spot, and they may turn you down instantly. Assure them that all you want is helpful information about their industry and company.) A second goal is to obtain the names of others you can talk with. Try this direct but diplomatic approach: "You've been extremely helpful. Could you tell me the names of others in your company or in the industry who could also give me a better understanding of this field?" Write down these names and companies in your Contact Notebook.
- Complete one or more Strategic Projects.
- Call two former bosses or supervisors tonight. After some brief "catch-up" talk, tell them you are looking for employment and would appreciate their advice and help:

1. If you've been away from the industry, ask them what changes have taken place that could affect someone in your field and position. This information can help you sharpen your resume and cover letters with more topical information.
2. Ask if they will give you a candid analysis of your strengths and weaknesses. Write these down. Ask if you can quote them in material you are sending out. "Strength" quotes from former bosses carry a lot of weight!
3. Ask them for names of individuals and companies you should contact. Don't write this information down on little slips of paper. Use your Contact Notebook.

Be sure to thank them. While you're thinking about it, send off a short note that repeats your thanks and enclose a copy of your resume. You now have at least two more people who know you are looking for a job and are aware of your qualifications.

Raise Questions to Increase Interest and Response

Start a good mystery book tonight. Mystery writers are masters at creating "page-turners." They do this by constantly planting questions in their readers' minds. "I watched Susan remove the small bottle from her purse. But then I glimpsed a tiny spot of blue that was the last thing on earth she ever wanted me to see . . ." You *have* to turn the page to find out what it was. Use this same technique when you send introductory letters to CEOs. For example, "Because I am interested in working for your company, I've talked with some of your customers about your company's particular strengths. I was surprised by what they felt was one of your organization's great unexploited strengths. I hope to share some of their comments with you when we meet." Think the CEO won't want to know what they said?

Use this same technique to force readers to go from your cover letter to your resume.

- **20-Minute Wake-up Exercise.** This morning, why not invite a neighbor to walk with you. Ask your neighbor if he or she belongs to any local groups or clubs that would be good places to meet new people. Would your neighbor sponsor you as a guest? Never be afraid to say you want to broaden your circle of friends to increase your employment opportunities. Hey, that's one of the ways Bill Clinton became President Bill Clinton, First Networker of the Land.
- **Media Review.** Read local newspapers for more names for your Job Prospect Cards. Circle all help-wanted ads for which you qualify. (If the job is clearly outside your area of experience, skip it. Effective time management requires that you always concentrate on prospects offering the best chance of success.)
- **Research.** Spend at least two hours in the library this morning. Read recent issues of *Standard & Poor's Outlook Reports*. While these reports are designed primarily for investors, they give you invaluable tips about which companies are rising stars and which have fallen on hard times. Make notes about all local companies for your Job Prospect Cards. Also, see the *Encyclopedia of Associations* and look up associations for your chosen industry. Photocopy these pages. Before you leave the library, check out a book about your industry for evening reading.
- Based on your newspaper reading and library visit, complete five Job Prospect Cards.
- Complete five or more Life Experience Cards.
- **Network!** Call each of the associations listed for your industry. Ask to speak to the executive director. You may not always get through to this individual, but when you start at the top you can always be referred to the next lower rung. During this call you want to find out:

1. If the association has a membership directory, and if you can get one free or at a modest cost. Ditto for a recent issue of their association newsletter.
2. Ask what particular problems that industry faces (business being lost to overseas companies, environmental problems, etc.).

This information can add muscle to your cover letters and resumes.

3. Ask for names of executives you should call for more information. Association execs usually know all the key players in their industry. A referral from an association official is money in the bank.

Write a letter to the CEO of each of the five new companies you've just added to your Job Prospect Cards. If you found an interesting item about the company in the newspaper, you can make your letter more topical if you refer to it (unless, of course, it involves corporate embezzlement).

This afternoon perform at least two of the Strategic Projects.

This evening call your minister, priest, or rabbi. Explain that you are currently looking for work and ask for suggestions. Often these religious leaders have contacts with hundreds of business-people. At the end of the conversation, why not suggest that the church or synagogue start a group for job seekers. Volunteer to help set up this group. Many religious and social organizations across the country are providing meeting places where members can share job leads and job-hunting tips.

Dream Some "Impossible Dreams"

Ask yourself how creative and enthusiastic you were today in your job search. Did you try some new ideas? Arthur Clarke said, "The only way to find the limits of the possible is by going beyond to the impossible."

DAY FIVE FRIDAY

- **20-Minute Wake-up Exercise.** Ask yourself: Which jobs have I enjoyed most in my life? Which of my projects seemed to win the most favorable attention from my bosses, clients, or co-workers? This should give you more entries for your Life Experience Cards.
- **Research.** While the subject of your morning thinking is fresh in your mind, complete at least five Life Experience Cards.
- **Media Review.** Read the local newspapers with marker in hand. Mark and clip stories about companies and people on your Job Prospect Cards. Don't worry about sorting these now; we'll suggest some ways to organize this information shortly. Just keep clipping! Mark all appropriate help-wanted ads. Don't forget to individualize your cover letter and resume in applying for those positions for which you are especially qualified.
- Complete at least five Job Prospect Cards.
- **Network!** Review your Contact Notebook and the names that you've gathered. Call any people you have not yet reached. Be sure to use the name of the person who referred you. Your goal for each call is to gather more information about a particular company or industry or to gather more names for your contact file.
- Write a letter to the CEO of each of the five new companies you've just added to your Job Prospect Cards. (Before you write these letters, review your stack of Life Experience Cards.) Do some of your resume statements seem particularly appropriate to one or more of these companies? If so, add them to your letters to these CEOs. Try your best to line up one or more informational interviews for next week.)
- Complete one or more of the Strategic Projects.
- Spend the afternoon on the road. Check a local map to plan your stops in certain areas of the city. Visit one or more employment agencies you have already contacted (most are accustomed to drop-in job hunters) and be sure to combine as many stops as you can to make the most of your time. Talk with a job counselor about prospects in your field. Show the counselor your resume and cover letter and ask for a candid critique. If

you're completely satisfied with their professionalism (see Chapter Nine), complete an application. Remember, this agent will represent you in talking with prospective employers. If he or she seems vague or unresponsive in a conversation with you, the agent may do an equally poor job of presenting you to the employer. Visit the personnel offices of some of the companies in your Job Prospect Card file. Ask to complete a job application.

* Do you belong to any local clubs or volunteer organizations? This evening call at least three fellow members. Ask them to candidly evaluate your past contributions to the organization. You may get some surprising third-party evaluations you can add to your Life Experience Cards. Tell them of your job search and ask if they know of any influential or knowledgeable businesspeople who might be in a position to help you. Add these names to your Contact Notebook and plan on calling them on Monday.

"You don't know our business . . ."

While you're lying in bed, start preparing yourself for the tough interview questions you may soon start facing. Some interviewers may say you don't have enough experience for the available job. You might mention Henry Ford's philosophy. "I suggest that you promote people who aren't experts in the operations they'll run. We do this all the time. Why? Because they don't know what can't be done. They challenge tradition, ignore artificial boundaries, and often discover that the impossible isn't impossible after all."

DAY SIX SATURDAY

- **20-Minute Wake-up Exercise.** Increase your pace to increase your blood flow. Ask yourself: Would I be willing to move to another city or country for the right job? Would uprooting my family be possible? The answers to these questions could help you determine how wide a net you cast in looking for employment.

- **Media Review.** Scan all morning newspapers. Clip, save, and respond. You probably know the routine by now. If you have decided to look beyond your city and its nearby vicinity, you should consult the *National Business Employment Weekly* (help-wanted ads reprinted from all regional editions of the *Wall Street Journal*; 800-562-4868) and/or the *National Ad Search* (help-wanted ads from 72 major U.S. newspapers; 800-992-2832). Remember that most of these ads are at least one week old when you see them. Respond immediately to any positions that sound appropriate.

- **Research.** Spend one or two hours at the public library today. You should be good friends with the reference librarian by now. Check the *Million Dollar Directory* for profits of top companies in your region. Read also *Standard & Poor's Register—Directors and Executives.* Review the periodical file for trade magazines in your industry and scan them for news about executive promotions and companies introducing new products. Note that some trade magazines also carry help-wanted ads.

- While you're at the library, complete at least ten Job Prospect Cards. Make them as complete as you can, with executive names, titles, company phone numbers, and addresses.

- Write a letter to each of the CEOs of these companies. Remember to add a strong close, something like "I will call you this week."

- Do at least one of the Strategic Projects that can be accomplished on a weekend.

- Review the various news clips about companies and your industry that you have gathered to date. Make a list of the problems these companies may be having (as reflected in the stories). Do these problems fall into any type of pattern? If so, share these insights when you write your CEO letters.

• Call members of your "Board of Advisers" (see Chapter 8) to review your initial job search and ask for advice.

Bedtime Reading

Scan recent issues of the *Wall Street Journal, Business Week,* and *Fortune.* These are good business overview magazines that can help you spot various trends in different industries, particularly problems facing many American companies. As you read, think about how your past experiences and skills could help contribute to solving these problems.

DAY SEVEN SUNDAY

- **20-Minute Wake-up Exercise.** Take a walk, jog, or ride a stationary bike. Ask yourself: Which of the companies I've marked as job prospects offer me the best chance for employment? Why do I think that? Which two companies would I prefer as employers? Why?
- **Media Review.** Read the local newspapers. Mark and clip news stories involving your job prospects and look for new companies to add. Pay special attention to the expanded business and classified help-wanted advertising sections that appear on Sundays. If you live in a small town, check local stores or newsstands for the Sunday editions of nearby major city newspapers.
- **Research.** Complete at least five Job Prospect Cards.
- Write a letter to the CEO of each of these five companies. Do not send a resume. Send another letter, with a resume, to the director of the human resources department.
- Complete at least five Life Experience Cards. This is your final day for this assignment. By now you should have accumulated a minimum of 35 cards. These will be invaluable to you in writing letters to companies, as it is essential to cite the most appropriate information from your cards. We suggest you keep a stack of these cards handy. Complete new cards whenever you remember pertinent past activities and achievements (or add new ones). This should be a continuing exercise throughout your career.
- Begin setting up manila file folders for each of the companies on your Job Prospect Cards. Clip your card to the top of the folder. Insert any news items or research notes you've gathered on these companies in the past week.
- Now select two of these companies as your *best* prospects. Put a prominent check mark by them. You are going to target these two companies for special attention in the week ahead.
- Review your Contact Notebook. Have you called all of the contacts you've gained from your networking? Have you called back everyone you were not able to reach the first time? Circle their names and add them to your tomorrow's "to do" list.
- This evening take in a movie or watch a re-run of "Cheers."

You've put in a hard week's work and you've earned some relaxation.

Goals for Your Second Week

- *Target two or more companies for special attention.*
- *Concentrate on lining up and completing several job or informational interviews this week.*
- *Sign agreements to work with at least three employment agencies. Be sure that each of these is an employer-paid-fee agency (rather than an applicant-paid-fee agency).*

DAY EIGHT MONDAY

- **20-Minute Wake-up Exercise.** Ask yourself: What basic skills do I have right now? Which of these are directly related to my occupational specialty, and which are transferable to other occupations? Special communication and "people" skills, for example, can be applied in many different fields.
- **Media Review.** Review the morning newspapers. Mark, clip, and save news items for your growing company files. Look particularly for information about the two companies you've targeted for special attention. Answer any appropriate help-wanted ads.
- **Network!** This morning, visit your local State Employment Office. Review the microfiche for any available jobs.
- Visit your local public library. You particularly want to look for information about your two targeted companies and their executives. If they are large publicly traded companies, look in Dun & Bradstreet's *Million Dollar Directory* and *Standard & Poor's Register of Corporations, Directors and Executives*. For smaller companies, ask the librarian about any state or local business directories that may be available. While you're in the library, spend a few minutes with one or more of the trade journals in your field. If one of the reference librarians has been particularly helpful, write a short note of praise about that person to the head librarian. This is not only a nice thing to do; it's a smart thing to do. The librarian's supervisor will undoubtedly show that person the letter. And you can expect a lot of friendly cooperation in the future.
- Call a number of local colleges and request copies for catalogs for next semester's classes (these catalogs are also often on file at your local library). Especially look for community colleges that offer courses taught by local businesspeople. Call some of the teachers if they are employed by companies you want to work for, and ask them for more information about their courses. (This is often a good introduction because they then might want to talk further about their industry.) Try to set up a personal interview with them for next week and ask for names of others in the same field you should talk with. Remember to record all this information in your Contact Notebook.

- **Research.** Complete at least five Job Prospect Cards.
- Write to the CEOs of these five companies. Try some variations on the opening of your letter. (Direct-mail companies constantly experiment with different types of letters and text until they find the most effective one.)
- Visit at least one of the two companies you've targeted for special attention. Take note of how the employees dress. Visit the human resources office and complete a job application (it certainly can't hurt, especially if they are currently looking). Also, obtain a copy of the annual report and pick up any advertising literature about the company that may be available in the lobby. Copy down the names and titles of executives listed on the directory in the lobby. If there is a general reception desk, ask for the names of the people who head the departments you want to work for. By now you should have gathered a great number of names and titles, and this will prepare you for the next step. Keep in mind, however that not every company, particularly financial institutions, welcomes "drop in" visitors. However, even these organizations will usually let you see the person or department who handles personnel. As we suggested earlier, you can also ask to see someone in public relations or investor relations.
- **Network!** This afternoon call several of the executives at your targeted companies. Tell them you are doing a special study of their company and would appreciate any information they can give you. Try to set up a personal 15-minute interview. Or ask if there is another person in the company you should talk with. Get more names. Yes, you will get some turn-downs. But if you remain cheerful and show a genuine interest in the company, you are bound to melt some stone hearts.
- Write to at least two of the managers or department heads at your two targeted companies. Remember that you can often find out who these people are simply by calling that department and asking for the name and title of the person in charge.
- **Follow-up.** Add these names/titles/phone extensions to your Contact Notebook. Whenever you're unable to reach one of them, circle that name to call later. Keep calling until you get through.
- Complete at least one of the Strategic Projects.

How do you impress other people?

Before you go to sleep tonight, think over the reactions of the various people you reached today. Did they spend time with you or try to cut you off? Did you run into an iron-eared gatekeeper who refused to put you through to the boss? What could you have done to increase their responsiveness to you?

Day Nine Tuesday

- **20-Minute Wake-up Exercise.** Ask yourself: What additional career skills may I need now and for future employment? A foreign language? Computer training? Ability to communicate more clearly? How can I attain these skills?
- **Media Review.** Review the local newspapers. These are still your best source of immediate information about new developments in your industry or specific companies. Really dig into the various sections. In the lifestyle section you might find an article about a woman who has developed a new diet program and is rapidly building a loyal local following. Sounds as if her company might need help. On the sports page you might see an article about executives playing in a golf tournament. Add their names and companies to your Job Prospect Cards. And add the notation "likes golf" to each name. If you are a fellow golfer, you have some raw material for "small talk" at the beginning of a phone conversation or a job interview.

  Review all the help-wanted ads. Have some been repeated from last week? This could indicate they are having trouble finding the right person. If you passed over these ads the first time because you felt your qualifications weren't perfectly appropriate, answer them now.
- **Research.** Complete at least five Job Prospect Cards.
- Write a letter to each of the CEOs on your new Job Prospect Cards. Perhaps you might mention golf in your letter to one of the presidents you saw teeing off in the newspaper this morning. Remember, you can build positive rapport by talking about what interests others—namely their businesses and, in this instance, their hobbies.
- Send a letter, with a resume, to the human resources director of these companies.
- **Network!** In your previous position, did you have direct contact with the firm's clients or customers? If so, call the people you dealt with. Because they are in the same industry, they can be a great resource. As clients or customers, their names could also open many doors at your prospective new firms. Don't overlook the possibility that the client's company could also have posi-

tions available now or in the immediate future. Be sure to ask the obvious: "What's happening at your company?" and "Whom should I talk with?"

• Try at least two of the Strategic Projects.

• Try something totally new. Remember in your former position how you were often asked to come up with a solution to a problem before 5 P.M.? We're going to ask you to do that now. You've been reading what others have done to network and get jobs in today's market. Think about how you could use your talents and experience to influence at least two people to interview you this week. Then *do it* this afternoon, before 5 P.M.

Attitude Check

How are you coming across in your phone calls and interviews? Are people responding to you, or do they seem remote? A number of "head hunters" have told us that some senior executives looking for work come across as arrogant and condescending, especially toward younger interviewers with much less experience than themselves. These execs are often totally unaware of their attitude. Remember Dale Carnegie's timeless advice: "You can make more friends in two months by becoming interested in them than you can in two years by trying to get others interested in you." This advice is key in building rapport with prospective employers.

- **20-Minute Wake-up Exercise.** Take a walk, jog, or ride a bike for 20 active minutes to get your blood circulating. Think about the day ahead. How many people can you network with today? How many hiring authorities can you talk with? All evidence shows that job hunters with the furthest reach and the greatest degree of optimism find employment much faster than those who stop frequently to rest or brood.
- **Media Review.** Read the local newspapers. Don't stop at the obvious. Try reading the society columns. You might read something useful, such as: "Mr. and Mrs. Charles Renfern from Ohio were recently welcomed to the community. Mrs. Renfern heads the new Customer Relations Department at Delman Department Stores." You now have a new executive's name and company name to add to your Job Prospect Cards, but you also have some other grist for your mill. You've learned that a new department has been formed. Perhaps they need additional help. Remember to respond to all appropriate help-wanted ads.
- **Research.** Schedule another visit to the public library. Are you finding the material you need at your local library? If not, consider visiting a larger regional library. Review some of the trade magazines in your industry. Of course, you'll want to check any help-wanted ads, but also be sure to check news about which companies are expanding, adding a new sales territory or factory. Personnel columns can tell you who is moving up or around. If they are involved with companies in your area, write down their names and new titles for your Job Prospect Cards.
- Complete at least five Job Prospect Cards.
- Write to the CEOs of each of these five companies. Tell him or her you will call for an interview shortly. Send another letter, with a resume, to the human resources director.
- **Follow-up.** Last week you wrote to some 30 CEOs. In each letter you indicated that you would call them. Start making those phone calls now. You have two goals: to get an interview and/or to get the names of others in the company you should talk with.
- **Network!** Call three or four insurance agents. Insurance agents are often so delighted to receive phone calls that they will talk

for a long time. They are also excellent sources for names of new executives and companies in town. They also usually know which companies are growing or cutting back. Tell them up front that you are looking for a position and would appreciate referrals. Ask them how they network with others. Insurance agents are often expert networkers.

- Try to reach department heads at the two companies you've targeted for special attention. Even if you're unable to get through today, write down their extension numbers. If they are out of town, ask their secretaries for the names and titles of people who handle their responsibilities while they're away. Now you have two names—the original exec to call back later and his or her assistant. Often the assistants are hiring authorities in their own right or can provide good background information about how the department works and the types of people they employ. As we've said before, if you show a genuine interest in the people you are calling, they will respond.
- Try at least one of the Strategic Projects.

"Script" Your Networking Meetings

We hope you have been able to line up one or two business mixers this week—a Chamber of Commerce breakfast or an introductory meeting at one of the service clubs such as Kiwanis, Lions, or Rotary. Take plenty of business cards with you and head for people you don't know. Tonight write a short "script" that you can use. For example: "Hi, I'm Bill Richards. I'm a consultant to purchasing departments. Tell me what you do." After a moment's conversation, make your key point. "I've decided to look for greater opportunities in the purchasing department of a progressive local company. Do you have any suggestions of companies I might contact?" If the individual supplies one or more company names, ask "Do you have any recommendations of people I should call at that company?" Tell people exactly what information you want at these networking meetings. Otherwise you probably won't get it.

DAY ELEVEN THURSDAY

- **20-Minute Wake-up Exercise.** Walk, jog, or bike ride. Ask yourself: Which of my friends have been the most successful in their careers? What qualities do they have that helped them succeed? Why don't I call them at home this evening and ask them about this?

- **Media Review.** Read the local newspapers and any state or local business magazines for leads about what changes in business are coming about. Which companies are doing the most aggressive advertising? Check the business calendar. Are there any local business meetings you should attend to practice your networking? Clip and save any pertinent articles in the appropriate company files.

- **Research.** Complete at least five new Job Prospect Cards. Include company names from your reading and those you've obtained from friends.

- Write to the CEOs of all five of those companies. Add any references from newspapers or from friends' comments about those companies that will make your letter seem more personal and less like a cookie-cutter form letter.

- Review all of your Job Prospect Cards. As of today, you should have at least 55 of them. Add any additional information you've gathered from your reading or phone conversation to make these cards more complete. Fax numbers can be particularly useful, as you will see from the next suggestion.

- If a company on your list has introduced a new product, opened a new store, or reported record profits, send a fax of congratulations to the CEO. Mention that you would be interested in working for such a progressive company, include a sentence about your experience, and ask whom you should contact. Yes, this may be the same CEO you wrote to last week, but you are becoming known. And most company execs are impressed by people who show gentle but continuing persistence, which is the same quality they often look for in prospective employees. Faxing is one of the most forceful ways you can send a message today. Some laws now prohibit sending "junk faxes" to companies you are not doing business with; however, it is unlikely that a company will complain about a one-page fax. Just don't send five pages. That's an irritant and ties up their machine.

- In addition to the two companies you have chosen for special attention, add a third today from among your Job Prospect Cards. Make your choice based on which company you feel would be most likely to hire you based on information you've been able to gather.

- **Network!** Call different department heads at your three targeted companies. Explain that you are currently researching the company because you are interested in working with them in the immediate future. Ask if they have time to answer just two questions (which you will have ready and are based on your research). Offer to call back if it is not a good time to talk. During the conversation, try to arrange a time to talk with them further "for fifteen minutes." If that is not possible, ask for the names of others in the company you should talk with. Then call those individuals, using the name of the person who just referred you. Names are magic when you're making cold calls.

- Complete at least two of the Strategic Projects.

- This evening, call those successful friends you were thinking about this morning. Ask them how they would go about finding employment in today's tight job market. Then, of course, ask them which companies and individuals they would suggest you contact. Add the names to your Contact Notebook and call these people tomorrow.

- **Follow-up.** Have you been successful in setting up any "informational" or job interviews this week or next? If not, call more of the CEOs you wrote to last week. Ask when it would be convenient for you to come see them or another executive they might suggest. Every call helps strengthen their memory of your name, but never press so hard that you fall into the "pest" category.

Does Your Correspondence Have a Coup de Theatre?

In advertising, you learn that you can't *bore* anyone into answering a direct response ad or letter—you must *surprise* the reader. Ad master David Ogilvy refers to this unexpected element as a *coup de theatre*. Does your letter start with a prosaic "I am interested in learning more about employment opportunities in your company"? CEOs instantly label these letters SEP—send to personnel. Or does your letter demand attention? "I didn't realize your company sold tractors in Indonesia until one of your clients told me about a wild ride at midnight on a rubber plantation." Collect anecdotes from your reading and networking conversations. Most executives love hearing stories about themselves, their companies, and their clients.

- **20-Minute Wake-up Exercise.** If you've been walking, today walk in a different direction. Ask yourself: How do I really appear to others? Should I lose five pounds? Get a haircut? It sounds like common-sense advice, but job counselors say that sometimes even seasoned executives let their grooming slip after several weeks at home.

- **Media Review.** Spend some time with the local papers. Begin to concentrate on those that give you the most usable data—good business coverage, extensive help-wanted classified section, and interesting stories about company executives. Clip and add appropriate articles to your various company folders. Respond to all help-wanted ads that match your qualifications and interests.

    Creative Edge: If there's a favorable story about a local company in which the CEO or one of the top managers was interviewed, call up the reporter. Ask him or her some questions that were not answered in the article. Then ask who should you talk with in the company for more information. The reporter will probably refer you to the person he interviewed. Then, when you call and ask for the CEO, name the reporter as the one who referred you. Your call should go right through!

- **Research.** Complete at least five Job Prospect Cards. Don't worry if the information is somewhat sketchy. Perhaps all you have is the name of the company and the location. Put it down. Call the company's personnel department to add the name of the company's CEO and the names of department heads. You can always add more information after your library visits and networking conversations.

- Write a letter to each of the CEOs of these companies. Close with a promise that you will call them next week. Add their names to your Contact Notebook.

- **Network!** Was there a coffee shop or favorite small restaurant near your former place of employment? Why not have lunch there and see if you can talk with former co-workers or bosses. They may not have much time to talk, but tell them that you are looking for employment and mention that you plan to call them for suggestions. Then call. *Bonus:* Sometimes returning to old haunts will remind you of people you have forgotten who might be valuable contacts.

- This afternoon, call some people with whom you've done business recently—a real estate agent, a lawyer, an accountant. Ask about new companies opening in town or taking additional real estate space. You want company and executive names, and your business relationship will usually persuade them to respond to your calls and provide you with leads.

    Creative Edge: Networking is a two-way street. Share information that is valuable to the people you call—for example, giving the real estate agent a tip about a family interested in selling their home or telling the accountant about new client prospects you may have uncovered in your job research.

- Complete two of the Strategic Projects.
- **Follow-up.** Review copies of your correspondence to CEOs last week. Were some out of town or unavailable when you called? Call them again today. Push hard to set up interviews for next week, either with them or someone they designate.
- Recheck employment agencies you've registered with. If you do not feel an agency is marketing your services aggressively, switch.

Be Ready for Surprise Phone Calls

Sometimes you may receive a call late in the evening. A friendly voice thanks you for your recent application and begins a general conversation with you. Don't be fooled into thinking this is just a routine call. In all probability it is a screening call, designed to reduce the number of applicants invited to an in-person interview. (Screening calls are frequently used by out-of-town companies that don't want to pay the travel expenses of a live interview unless the person is fully qualified.) Answer each of the caller's questions as carefully as you would in an actual interview. Use this call to find out as much as you can about the position—what your exact duties would be, who you would report to within the company, etc. The more you learn, the better your in-person interview will be. Write down the name, title, and phone number of the person you're talking with. If you "pass" this interview, there is a strong possibility you'll be invited to come in for a face-to-face interview.

DAY THIRTEEN SATURDAY

- **20-Minute Wake-up Exercise.** By now, you're probably settling into this routine and beginning to enjoy it. Ask yourself: What types of questions will I probably face in a tough job interview? How will I handle questions about problems in my past or long gaps between jobs when I was unemployed or ill?

- **Media Review.** Read the local newspaper and one or two trade magazines. What's the general outlook for business in your community or in your industry specialty? Which companies are making waves? Clip and file every article that mentions one of your job prospects, especially those you've targeted for special attention.

- **Network!** Your telephone is your most efficient networking tool. Spend most of today calling friends and acquaintances, making notes about companies and contacts they recommend. You probably know many more people than you realized.

  Here are a few ways to recall their names:

  - Check your Christmas card list, which is usually a bonanza of names and addresses, including old friends you haven't talked with in years.
  - Look for your old company's phone book. In some instances you may have jotted down home phone numbers of key personnel whom you worked with regularly.
  - Check your old Rolodex.
  - Review social and business correspondence from the past year.

Record these names and phone numbers in your Contact Notebook. Then check off each person as you call them.

As you're getting reacquainted, ask about other mutual friends you've had and where they are today. Get their names and phone numbers for your growing network list, then ask your key questions:

- What companies would you recommend I contact?
- Do you know of any individuals within those companies

who could give me more information about their organization and job possibilities?

- May I use your name when I call them?

"Man's best friend, aside from the dog, is the waste basket"— Business Week magazine

Because you've been gathering information on many different companies and people these past two weeks, your files may be scattered all over your desk—and everywhere else in your home. This evening, refile everything that is out of place. If you wrote down information on little slips of paper during the week, transfer all important information to your Contact Notebook. If material isn't pertinent or is redundant, throw it away.

DAY FOURTEEN SUNDAY

- **20-Minute Wake-up Exercise.** Do whatever you like to get the blood and creative juices flowing. Think about the past seven days of this program. What has worked (gotten a good response from an executive)? Has your personal networking at meetings been effective? Have you been getting past the various gate-keepers that guard their bosses' time or have you been running into walls?

- **Media Review.** Since this 14th day falls on a Sunday, spend a good part of the day doing research with the local newspapers. If you live within 300 miles of a metropolis such as New York, Boston, Chicago, Miami, or Los Angeles, buy a copy of that city's Sunday paper. Be aware that some major papers delete the help-wanted classified sections from papers delivered outside of their normal circulation area. However, the papers are still valuable because of their large business sections, which may also contain display help-wanted ads. Ask a friend who lives or works in one of those cities to send you the classified section for later review.

    Look for articles about your industry and especially about each of your job prospect companies. You may find useful information throughout these papers, sometimes in the most surprising places, like the society page, which we've mentioned, and the business page, where you might read: "Mr. Arnold Swenner has just been named Director of Sales Training for the Quartile Computer Company. . . ." If you're looking for a similar position, why not write a note of congratulation to Mr. Swenner and ask him if he'd been looking for a position for a while, and if he'd mind sharing his contact notes with you? This could save you hours of research time and costs Mr. Swenner nothing but a few minutes to help a fellow sales trainer. What makes this type of networking so effective is that the person you contact now knows your name and anticipates that he or she may need *your* help some day!

    Clip and file every relevant article. Keep looking for items about executives in your target companies that you can use in the first paragraph of your letters to them.

- **Research.** Complete at least five Job Prospect Cards.
- Write letters to the CEOs of each of those companies.
- **Network!** Use the afternoon for "soft" networking calls to friends and colleagues you weren't able to reach during the week. Your goal is to gather more names and information about companies you are researching. Even if they don't know anyone in your industry, ask them about their personal reaction to companies in that industry and anything they know about their products or services. Write down relevant quotes. Sometimes you can use these quotes in a letter to gain the immediate attention of a CEO or other hiring authority. For example, "One of your loyal customers told me this morning that she feels the new formulation of your dishwasher liquid, Cleer, is twice as effective as the old Cleer." Now you have the CEO's attention. Use it to tell him what added value you can bring to his progressive company.

Set Goals for the Third Week of Your Job Search

Here are some recommendations:

1. Add two more "special attention" companies to my target list.
2. Call every CEO or department head I've written in the past two week. Try to arrange a face-to-face interview.
3. Attend one or more local networking events.
4. Constantly refine and improve written correspondence and networking techniques. Change or drop techniques that don't seem to be working.

Other personal goals: (You fill these in.)

_____

_____

DAY FIFTEEN MONDAY

- **20-Minute Wake-up Exercise.** If you haven't been exercising regularly until you started this program, you may have started to notice an improvement in your muscle tone. You should have more energy for your job search this week. During your exercise, think about your current attitude. Do I really try to be courteous to everyone I meet in my job search? What is the attitude of secretaries when I try to reach their bosses? Do I treat them as equals who are trying to do their job, or do I become hostile if they don't put me through?

- **Media Review.** Review all the local newspapers. By now you should have started collecting trade magazines from your industry. If your search is national in scope, you will also want to check out the *National Business Employment Weekly* and the *National Ad Search*. Clip and file every article about your industry or your job prospects. Answer every appropriate help-wanted ad.

- **Research.** Select two more target companies for special attention. You now should have a total of five, which represent your best prospects.

- Visit one of these target companies today. Your stops should include human resources (put in an application), investor relations (pick up an annual report), and the directory in the lobby (take down department head names and titles). Also talk to any receptionist in the lobby for the names of different department heads.

- If time and proximity permit, visit a second company you've targeted. Repeat the above-listed activities.

- Spend some time at the public library. Use the library computers to research specific data (from magazine articles and books) about the two new target companies. Use the microfiche readers to check recent newspaper articles about them. Scan the Standard Stock Reports (*Standard & Poor's*) for names of "rising stars" (growing, profitable companies) in your area. Ask the reference librarian to recommend good local business directories.

- While you're in the library, use their research facilities to complete at least five more Job Prospect Cards.

- Complete at least two of the Strategic Projects. If one or more of the projects you tried last week yielded good results, repeat them. *The marketplace always tells you what works.*
- **Network!** Call several executives of both targeted companies you visited. Tell them you are researching their company in the interests of future employment. Ask them about their own careers with the company—for example, how they got ahead. If you've caught them at a quiet moment, you might get some very useful information—in fact, try calling during the lunch hour. In these difficult times, more and more executives are eating pastrami on rye at their desk, and they have more time to talk, especially about themselves. Ask if you can come in for a brief face-to-face talk. Then ask for names of others in the company who could help you with your research.
- **Follow-up.** Review your Contact Notebook and correspondence sheets. Check those people you were unable to reach by phone last week. Check additional names of execs who have had your letter in hand for at least a week. Make all those calls and record the results. If you have had any interviews, always write thank-you notes the day after.
- Write a letter to the CEO of your two new targeted companies. Use a creative opening based on your research. Ask a question or make a point, but don't be afraid to be provocative—without, of course, being offensive. You *must* do something to leave a distinct impression, capture that executive's attention, and cut through the clutter.

Be Nice to Everyone (You Never Know)

One personnel director of a major nonprofit organization plays a dirty trick on thoughtless job hunters. Once each day she takes the place of the receptionist in her office for about an hour to observe how job candidates might treat someone they consider beneath them. Some become irritable. One said, "Look, I don't have time to wait. I don't see you doing a damn thing about calling the personnel director. Why don't you do your job?"

After a pause, the "receptionist" stands up and introduces herself as the personnel director. "It lets me see a whole other side of people," she said.

Time Out: You're Now Halfway Through Your 30-Day Program

Do you feel discouraged?

Have you made dozens of phone calls, sent out almost 100 letters and applications, and feel nothing is happening?

You may have thoughts such as:

- What on earth am I doing all this for?
- No one is going to hire me.
- I'm too old.
- My salary expectations are too high.
- They won't want to fund my pension.
- I'm too young. I don't have enough experience.

This self-doubt can not only drag you down, it could even force you to abandon the program.

But we don't think you will.

You're doing your job, and as you contact more and more people, chances are you will encounter more rejection. Many people would quit this program now—it's like being on a diet for 15 days only to have the scale creep up two pounds.

But you're not going to drop out because you know the consequences of inactivity.

Day Sixteen Tuesday

- **20-Minute Wake-up Exercise.** While you're exercising, ask yourself: What kind of response have I had from the companies I've targeted for special attention? Informational interviews? Job interviews? Any other response? Ask yourself what you can do to stir things up.
- **Media Review.** Review all local newspapers. This can still be the most productive way to track new developments regarding companies and local help-wanted advertising. You know what to do by now—clip and file news items by company or industry and answer all appropriate ads.

   Before sending out your responses to ads, do a final quality check. Do your letters still sound enthusiastic? Do they immediately reach out and grab the reader? Do they promise a value-added benefit? If not, you may want to rewrite the opening of your cover letter. Does your letter *really* reflect what you can offer the company in view of their stated requirements in the ad? Look at your resume. Review your Life Experience Cards. Could you make your resume stronger for this particular job? If so, you may want to customize this cover letter and resume for this job. The extra effort is worthwhile if you really want this job and feel you are especially qualified for it.
- **Research.** Complete five more Job Prospect Cards. As of today, you should now have at least 80 companies on file. If not, add some names.
- Complete at least two of the Strategic Projects. Remember to repeat those that are working.
- Visit one of the two new companies you've targeted for special attention. Stop by the organization's personnel office. Ask for a job application. Check any bulletin board that lists current openings. Take notes on any that sound like you. If the company is publicly traded, drop by the investor relations office and pick up an annual report. Ask to speak to the person in charge of this office; such people are often very public relations oriented and may have time to give you some insight about the company. If you establish rapport, they may also recommend people you should see within the company. Pick up any adver-

tising literature or brochures about the company that may be on display, and before you leave, take note of how most employees dress. This information will be useful when you come for interviews. In just one visit, you can return with a whole file full of information on your targeted company.

- **Follow-up.** Review your Contact Notebook for names of any individuals you have not been able to reach. Try again now. Your goals for each call remain the same. Try to arrange a face-to-face meeting (either an informational or job interview). Obtain additional information about the organization. Finally, get additional names of hiring authorities you can call. *Personal contact is the key to getting hired. The more people you see each week, the faster you will be hired.*

- **Network!** Call recently retired executives you've met at parties or other gatherings. You especially want to talk with individuals from your industry or occupational specialty. Many of them now have time to talk and are flattered to be asked for advice. If they have retired in the last several years, they usually know many people who are still working at their old companies. They can provide you with names to contact. They may also be willing to call ahead to recommend you and set up your call. Be sure to ask recent retirees if they have an old company phone book. Many may have taken one with them when they left. This book is a gold mine of contacts, complete with extension numbers.

- This evening call friends, former co-workers, former bosses, etc., whom you were unable to reach previously. Also call members of your "Board of Advisers" to give them a progress report and ask for suggestions.

Thank You, Thank You, Thank You

Following an interview, send thank-you notes to the individuals who interviewed you as well as to others in the company who facilitated the meeting. One out-of-town interviewee sent a thank-you note to the company chauffeur who picked him up at the airport. The chauffeur was so pleased that he dropped in every few days to the personnel office to ask if "that nice man had gotten the job." It's great to have allies in the company.

- **20-Minute Wake-up Exercise.** Why not take a brisk walk this morning? Ask yourself: Have I acquired the additional career skills I need to compete in the current job market? Computer training? A communication and letter-writing course? Public speaking? If not, perhaps I'd better get moving!
- **Media Review.** Review the local newspapers. These are still the best source of immediate information about new industry developments. For example, in the lifestyle section you might find an article about a woman who has started a new business developing customized software for local companies. Do you have some technical or marketing expertise that could be helpful to her? Call her up. On the sports page you might see an article about executives playing in a charity tennis tournament. Add their names and companies to your Job Prospect Cards along with the notation "likes tennis." If you also are a tennis player, you have some raw material for small talk at the beginning of a phone conversation or a job interview.

  Review all the help-wanted ads. Remember, ads repeated from last week could mean the company is having trouble finding the right person. If you passed over these ads the first time because you feared you weren't qualified, answer them now.
- **Research.** Complete at least five Job Prospect Cards.
- Write a letter to each of the CEOs on your new Job Prospect Cards. Use a tennis analogy in your letter to the executive you saw serving the ball in the morning newspaper. You can build rapport by talking about what interests others—namely their businesses and, in this instance, their tennis game.
- **Network!** Many banks, county governments, and other organizations in your region may stage economic and other briefing meetings and breakfasts for local businesses. When you see these listed in the newspapers, call to see if you can get an invitation. These meetings are excellent places to met CEOs and dozens of other hiring authorities.
- Try at least two of the Strategic Projects.

Another Way Around the Gatekeeper

If you reach a CEO's secretary or administrative assistant and want to impress him or her with your "status" (so the person will put you through to the boss), ask your spouse or a friend to place the call as if he or she were your secretary. Then you can take over the phone when you're switched to the boss.

- **20-Minute Wake-up Exercise.** Try something different. If you have a portable cassette player with ear phones, listen to your favorite music as you exercise. Sometimes creative job-getting ideas may come when you least expect them, even in the midst of Beethoven's Fifth.
- **Media Review.** Read all the local newspapers for any news about every company on your list. Respond to appropriate help-wanted ads.
- **Research.** Complete at least five Job Prospect Cards. Starting to run dry of names? Why not call several local stock brokers. They can recommend some companies that are growing rapidly in the area. After all, it's their job to know. And don't worry—you have only 10 more of these cards to complete.
- **Network!** Call at least one executive at all five of your specially targeted companies. As in your previous calls, tell them you are researching the company for possible employment. Ask questions about the types of jobs that become available from time to time. Ask who in the company can provide more information. Try to arrange a personal informational interview.
- Call the employment agencies you've registered with. When you reach the person who is handling your account, check on its status.
- As of today, you have a universe of at least 90 organizations in your job prospect file. You have folders on each of them, with much fatter folders on the five companies targeted for special attention. Send a follow-up letter to each of the CEOs who has not responded to your previous letters. (You can see now why we suggested you work with a secretarial service or a willing spouse!)

Tape Record Key Points

After you set up a job interview, review all the notes in
your job prospect file on that company. Read some of
the news items and information from the annual report
aloud into a tape recorder. Now record key points
about your background and what added value you can
bring to that company. On your way to the interview,
play back this tape.

DAY NINETEEN FRIDAY

- **20-Minute Wake-up Exercise.** Take a walk, jog, swim, or do whatever activity you feel like. Clear your mind. Ask yourself: Am I building a network of people I can rely on not only now but also in the future? Do I show a real interest in the people I contact? Do I send them a thank-you note when they give me contact names? Am I committed to helping them should they need it in the future?
- **Media Review.** Read newspapers and trade magazines. Look for articles written by executives of companies you are researching. Photocopy each article and send a copy along with the letter you send to the executives. Add your own appreciative, thoughtful comments in the margins of the article copy, then add a note about your interest in knowing more about his or her organization. Almost every item and article in a trade magazine could represent a hidden job. If a company has increased its production run, it may need more managers or purchasing agents. If an S&L institution is restructuring, it may need accounting assistance and computer help. If a hospital is starting a fund-raising drive, perhaps your experience in sales training could help them motivate a group of inexperienced volunteers. Make your regular check of all help-wanted ads.
- **Research.** Visit your second home, the library. Your goal today is to complete your research on your five targeted companies and come up with five additional organizations for your Job Prospect Cards. Are you remembering to concentrate at least 70 percent of your efforts on companies with 100 or less employees? That's where real job creation is today.
- Complete at least five Job Prospect Cards.
- Write to the CEOs of each of those companies. While much of your letter can be boilerplate, your opening paragraphs should target the individual executive and the company's needs. This is where your research and reading can really pay off and give you the essential marketing edge. For example: "I applaud your efforts to hold down production costs with a new form of just-in-time inventory control. In my own experience in manufacturing, etc."

- Complete at least two of the Strategic Projects.
- **Network!** Call at least one additional executive at each of your five targeted companies. Try hard to arrange an informational interview next week. At the beginning of the conversation, mention not only the names of others in the company you've talked with but some of the company subjects you've talked about. For example: "Clyde Barnon in public relations was telling me about the new competition your products face from plants in Thailand." The more you establish yourself as a company "insider," the longer the person you call may be willing to talk. It's also a good way to build rapport for a future interview. At the end of the conversation, ask for the names of other people within the company you should contact.
- This evening call some fellow job seekers. Ask them what seems to be working for them. If you're not competing for the same types of jobs, consider swapping information about companies and job leads.
- **Follow-up.** By now your Contact Notebook should be filled with names and phone numbers. Today try to reach everyone you were unable to contact before. Your goal is to get information, more contact names, and most of all, that interview!

The Importance of Feeling Important

Remember the simple truth uttered by American philosopher John Dewey—that one of our deepest urges is the "desire to feel important." Cater to that universal need every time you write or call hiring authorities. Ask for their advice. Respect their experience and expertise. They'll respect you for your good judgment.

DAY TWENTY SATURDAY

- **20-Minute Wake-up Exercise.** Have you started to notice a difference in the way you feel? Vigorous exercise is a great antidote for depression, and everyone looking for a job today experiences feelings of depression sometimes. Ask yourself: Who am I? What does my career mean to me? Is it how I define myself?
- **Media Review.** Review local and national newspapers and trade magazines. Spend the morning reading and rereading them. Something important you missed the first time could jump out at you. Many communities now have weekly or monthly publications devoted entirely to local business news. These newspapers or magazines are filled with executive names and reports on organizational changes. Clip and file in your growing job prospect files. Answer all appropriate help-wanted ads.
- **Research.** Complete at least five more Job Prospect Cards. Congratulations! You have now gathered the names of at least 100 organizations that you would like to work for, and you have designated five of these companies as special targets. By now your files on these five should be bulging with articles, notes from telephone calls, and copies of your correspondence.
- If you have not received a response from the CEOs of the targeted companies you wrote to, write another letter today. Include some of the facts that surprised you about the company, and don't bother to refer to your previous letter, which the CEO may never have seen if it was intercepted by a gatekeeper. This time, include a one-page "questionnaire" with three (no more) questions about the company. Include a stamped, self-addressed envelope. For example:

Dear Executive:

I am currently completing an extensive research project on Staley Manufacturing Company. It seems to be the type of company I would want to work for now or in the future. However, because it is a privately held corporation, there is some information I have been unable to get. Answers to these three questions would be of great help to me. (Stamped, self-addressed envelope enclosed.)

Sincerely,
Your Name

Come up with two good questions for the survey based on your research of the company. Then add this third question: Who would be the best person in the organization to talk with regarding a position in your occupational specialty?

* Complete at least two Strategic Projects.
* **Network!** This evening try some "soft" networking. Go to a church supper, a community concert, or a friend's party. Look especially for new faces and introduce yourself. (Who knows, they may have just been brought into town by a company that's expanding.) Job seekers today have to be part Dale Carnegie, part CIA agent.

Getting Through

Do reporters use "tricks of the trade" when they are trying to reach a reclusive executive? Paul Plawin says, "Sometimes you just have to make dozens of phone calls. I have found that dogged persistence works best."

- **20-Minute Wake-up Exercise.** Perhaps try a different exercise this morning. Shoot baskets at a nearby playground. Ask yourself: "What are my transferrable skills? What have I learned to do in previous jobs that would be applicable—and valuable—to positions in other industries?

- **Media Review.** Buy all local Sunday newspapers, including papers from nearby major cities. Spread the sections out on the living room floor and go through each carefully. You will find executive names and company doings everywhere. Are there any upcoming jobs fairs listed? Any business breakfasts, public seminars, or speeches by local executives described in a community calendar? Which should you attend to network? Read the sports pages. See someone from a local college awarding a trophy? See an exec parading her pet at a dog or cat show? Clip and file. You have some great information for the beginning of your letters to them.

  You should have a wide variety of help-wanted ads to choose from. Remember that display ads sometimes appear in sections other than the classifieds, particularly in the business, sports, editorial, and education pages. Answer each ad for which you feel qualified. Send applications to companies in your industry who are advertising for people outside of your occupational specialty. The ads are an indication they are expanding and may soon need someone like you.

- **Research.** Spend a quiet day reviewing every letter you have sent out in the previous 20 days. Show them to your spouse or a business friend whose judgment you trust. Ask for honest answers. Are the letters interesting? Do they immediately attract the attention of the reader by focusing on something of potential importance to him or her? Are the letters free of business jargon? Do they lead logically to your request for more information, the names of other contacts in the company, or an informational interview?

  After listening to your reader's comments and considering your own reaction to the correspondence, you may want to rewrite some of the boilerplate text to make it more arresting and informative. Professional writers know that their material *always* gets better when it's rewritten after several days' respite.

- Set your goals for the important fourth week to come.
- Tonight make a fabulous dinner. Rent a movie. Pet the dog. The President of You, Inc., deserves a break. Just don't turn off the phone.

Your "Best Gift"

"One of the best gifts you have to offer when you write personal history is the gift of yourself. Don't forget it's there and that it has great power. Give yourself permission to write about yourself. And have fun doing it."

—*On Writing Well,* by William Zinser

Day Twenty-Two Monday

- **20-Minute Wake-up Exercise.** Ask yourself: What problems are my five targeted companies facing today? What problems is the whole industry facing? What problem-solving skills can I offer them?
- **Media Review:** Read the local papers and trade magazines. These are your daily lifelines to what is happening in the business world today that could affect your employment search. Are there headlines about a major company laying off people? That means fewer people will be applying for jobs there at a time when the company may have downsized too rapidly and may suddenly need someone with your skills. Pay attention to every company that is advertising for help—it's a sign of growth. Add these companies to your job prospect list. Remember to look for news about smaller companies, where so much of the hiring activity is concentrated today.
- **Research.** Complete at least five more Job Prospect Cards.
- Run through all 100-plus Job Prospect Cards. Has there been any recent news that would justify moving one or more of these companies to your special attention category?
- **Network!** Concentrate today on your five target companies. Call back anyone on your contact list that you were unable to reach. Try hard to arrange a face-to-face interview with each of your calls. Then try to add more names to your contact list for each of these companies. In the case of large companies you should have written to the CEO, Director of Human Resources, and at least five different hiring authorities in areas you want to work in. With smaller companies (fewer than 100 employees) you should have written or called the CEO and the Director of Personnel/Human Resources, which in smaller companies could be the president or another top executive who wears several hats, and at least two hiring authorities in areas you're interested in.
- Is there any afternoon or evening function you could attend—a meeting of a political party, a PTA gathering, a Lion's or Kiwanis club function? Each of these offers an opportunity to meet and talk with hiring authorities. If some are too busy to talk,

take their cards and make a mental note to call them later. The fact that you attended the same function gives you another chance to get past the executive gatekeepers. For example, you might say to the secretary, "I was talking with Mr. Kreisler at the Rotary Club last night and wanted to make a comment about some of his interesting remarks. Is he available now?"

- Complete at least two of the Strategic Projects. You're getting to be an old pro at this by now.
- Write a short note to each of the employment agencies you've signed with. In it, review the status of your job search today. Include some comments about particular companies and their attitude toward current hiring. This makes your letter more interesting and helpful to the agencies' job counselors. By helping to improve their efficiency, you become a friend and move closer to the top of their mind when they receive a call from an organization looking for someone like you.

Networking Works

Hal Gieseking told a lifelong friend from college days, Richard Janssen, then a senior editor at *Business Week,* that he was looking for additional work in writing. A few days later Mr. Janssen attended a presentation dinner at the World Trade Center and sat next to Peggy Burton, at that time a marketing supervisor for American Express. She told him about one of her principal jobs, developing the monthly American Express Cardmember newsletter. Dick said, "I know a writer you might want to meet . . ." One dinner and two meetings later, Hal took over all of the writing for the Cardmember newsletter for eight profitable years from the side porch of his home in Bronxville, New York. Networking can work for you 24 hours a day.

DAY TWENTY-THREE TUESDAY

- **20-Minute Wake-up Exercise.** The activity is your choice. Ask yourself: How many new people have I contacted or met in the last 22 days? Which of them did I like the most? Which the least? Why? Can I use some of the qualities I admire most in them in my own job interviews, correspondence, and phone calls?
- **Media Review.** Review the local newspapers. This is still an essential step. Because of the number of organizations on your job prospect list, you are probably noticing more news items that affect "your" companies. Clip those tidbits and save them in the appropriate files.

  You will also notice that you are almost unconsciously beginning to "chunk" related information in your mind. Almost all writers notice this helpful phenomenon when they do extensive research on a series of related subjects. Diverse ideas naturally begin to cluster together. Study these patterns to give you special and original insights that you can use in your correspondence and calls to various organizations. Of course, review and answer any appropriate help-wanted ads.
- **Research.** Spend some time at the library. If the reference librarian has been especially helpful these past few weeks, why not bring him or her a small gift of appreciation.

  Today try something a little different. Ask the librarian if he or she knows of any books or recent articles written by local business executives. Then scan these books or articles and make some notes. You now have an excellent reason to write to each of the authors and compliment them on their work. (Complimentary notes about an individual's projects are almost always passed on immediately to execs by their gatekeepers.) This initial letter helps you establish a relationship for future correspondence and phone calls. You are now a known quantity.
- Complete at least five Job Prospect Cards.
- Write a letter to each of the CEOs of those companies.
- **Network!** Have you written or called everyone who could hire you at your five targeted companies? Every department head . . . every supervisor . . . every company officer? Of course, you haven't! Keep calling and writing, constantly adding more

names. Don't worry about overcalling any one company. You're a fresh voice to every new executive you call. They don't know you've already talked with 20 other people at that company! And you may be surprised to find that with each call you actually become more comfortable because your research and previous conversations almost make you part of their team.

• Complete at least two Strategic Projects. Why not try a few "long shots" today? While we keep urging you to spend most of your time on those projects that put the odds in your favor, we all know that sometimes perennial seventh-placers can still win the Kentucky Derby.

Use Names

Dale Carnegie said, "Remember that a person's *name* is to that person the sweetest and most important sound in any language."

Using a person's name can warm some of the "coldest calls." But be conservative. Refer to the person as "Mr. Shaeffer" or "Mrs. Cloman." Some people are offended when strangers call them by their first name.

A simple reminder: Write the name of the interviewer or executive you are meeting with across the top of your note pad. Whenever you refer to your notes, you can refresh your memory of the individual's name and use it frequently in your conversation.

DAY TWENTY-FOUR WEDNESDAY

- **20-Minute Wake-up Exercise.** Tomorrow you start the last seven days of this program. Ask yourself: What progress have I made to date? What income alternative plans—such as temp work—should I consider to take care of my expenses?
- **Media Review.** Read the local newspapers. This morning try a column-by-column review of each section of all newspapers in the area. Since you now have at least 120 job prospects, several may be mentioned in the news. Check the stock market pages. Are the stocks of your companies going up or down? Look at the insider trader column. Are certain corporate executives buying up large quantities of stock? That could be a hint of profitability or expansion, long before any concrete news hits the papers. This section can also provide you with names and titles of key executives.
- **Research.** Complete five more Job Prospect Cards. Are at least 70 percent of your selections small companies?
- Write a letter to the CEO of each of these companies.
- Review all contacts made to date with each of your five targeted companies. Has each phone call or interview given you a better understanding of the company, its goals, income, and recent track record in the industry? Use this information when you call some of the mid-level executives at each of these companies. They'll be impressed by your understanding of the company and by your insight.
- **Network!** Contact all local businesspeople with whom you have a working relationship: lawyers, accountants, and insurance reps. Ask again about which companies are expanding. Ask for their opinions of the five companies you've targeted for special attention. Their comments could make great quotes in your letters to individuals at these five organizations.
- Ask friends and former colleagues to recommend some good temp agencies if you are willing to accept part-time work.

Reading More in Less Time

As Henry Steel Commager wrote, "Every society needs a constant flow of new ideas." So do job hunters. A constant flow of new ideas helps make you more competitive in the job market. And you must read a great deal of material when you research individual companies and industries. Here are two ways to make your reading more efficient:

- *Delegate reading assignments.* Ask a willing spouse, family member, or friend to help you scan newsletters, articles, etc. Give your helper an outline of the kind of information you're looking for and ask them to write a brief summary of what they find.
- *Listen to industry and business news on your car cassette player.* Newstrak Executive Tape Service supplies summaries of current business and management reports from leading publications; for more information call 800-525-8389. For good, brief monthly summaries of the key ideas in current business books, subscribe to Soundview Executive Book Summaries; for more information call 800-521-1227.

Day Twenty-Five Thursday

- **20-Minute Wake-up Exercise.** If you've been walking faithfully, you've probably noticed it in your increased endurance. As you walk, ask yourself: How am I coming across in job interviews? Do I always ask the interviewer to summarize the key responsibilities of the person taking the position? Have I been summarizing my past experiences with those responsibilities in mind?
- **Media Review.** Review the newspapers. These are still the best daily source of late-breaking information about local companies. The enterprising reader may find job leads in the most unusual places. Is an owner advertising a home for sale? Are they moving to another area and giving up their present job? It doesn't hurt to call and ask. Are any job fairs or trade shows coming to your area? These are perfect hunting grounds for networking. As always, continue to look for help-wanted ads as well as every single item written about your growing list of job prospects.
- **Research.** Complete at least five Job Prospect Cards. Are you getting stuck for new names? Call your local chamber of commerce and ask for the names of their five newest members. These companies could be expanding or new to the area, either of which could mean they might require additional personnel.
- Write a letter to the CEOs of each of these five companies.
- **Network!** If you have not yet personally visited the headquarters of your five targeted companies, arrange visits today and tomorrow. In large companies, stop by the human resources office, the public relations office, and the investor relations office. Pick up company literature wherever you go and read every bulletin board. Look for posted job openings, notices of promotions, and awards or announcements of new contracts. In smaller companies ask if you can see the president, marketing director, or person in charge of a department you want to work for. Sometimes the pressure of your presence in the lobby can motivate an executive to see you for a few minutes.
- Complete at least two Strategic Projects.
- **Follow-up.** Write thank-you notes to everyone who interviewed you or who let you interview them about the company. If ap-

propriate, enclose a revised resume that reflects new things you learned about the company during the interview.

Networking Phone Strategies

Here is another technique to get past the gatekeepers and talk with one of the company's major executives.

Secretary: "May I ask why you're calling Mrs. Hartley?"

You: "Yes, I would appreciate her comments about (name of a competitive company). I promise to keep her remarks in confidence."

Many executives love to talk about their competition. During the conversation, you can mention that you are researching that particular industry in the interests of future employment.

Alternative: Ask for their opinion about one of the companies they do business with (one of your targeted companies). You also could ask for names of people within that company you should call. Now you have a referral from a customer: "Mrs. Haymes of Hartman Industries gave me your name." Few supervisors or department heads will ignore a customer's implied request for their attention.

DAY TWENTY-SIX FRIDAY

- **20-Minute Wake-up Exercise.** Ask yourself: What contributions do I make to community causes? What volunteer activities have I participated in this past year?
- **Media Review.** Review local newspapers. Read any trade magazines and newsletters that have accumulated during the week. Clip and file by company or industry every relevant article or item. Answer any appropriate help-wanted ads.
- **Research.** Complete at least five Job Prospect Cards. For other sources of names try *America's Corporate Families,* published in two volumes annually by Dun & Bradstreet Information Service and listing over 67,000 branches and divisions of major American corporations with names and titles of major executives; it's available at major libraries.
- Review the files of your five targeted companies, including your notes from conversations with all hiring authorities. By now you should have a pretty comprehensive picture of them. Using this information, write another letter to the CEO of each company, with a copy to each of the supervisors and department heads you've talked with along the way. Summarize the findings of your research. Tell them you are now more convinced than ever (if indeed you are) that you want to work for their firm. End with a question, such as: "What can I do to convince you that I would be a real asset to your organization? I will call you next week for the answer." Stay in the driver's seat. Never say, "Please call me"—always say, "I will call you."
- Complete at least two Strategic Projects.
- **Network.** Check in with the various members of your board of advisers. Report your progress to date. What has been working for you? What hasn't? Do they have any suggestions for you? Have they recently met someone you should contact for more information?
- **Follow-up.** Today is round-up day for most of this week's networking. Try to bring your pending requests for job and informational interviews to a close. Call at least one person at each of your five targeted companies.

Community Involvement Pays Off

When Steve Blanks, president of Crestar Bank in the
Williamsburg area of Virginia, interviews candidates for
a job, he often finds that many candidates for banking
positions have top credentials. "But then I try to probe
deeper. I ask them to describe their work ethic. And
then I ask a key question: What have they done in the
past for the communities they've lived in."

Day Twenty-Seven Saturday

- **20-Minute Wake-up Exercise.** What's your favorite exercise? Go to it! Ask yourself: Have I really accepted the TQM (Total Quality Management) concept in my life? Do I communicate this dedication to quality in each phone call I make and letter I write?
- **Media Review.** Read the local newspapers. By now you probably reach for the scissors every time you reach for a newspaper. Clip and file any relevant information in your growing files. Answer any appropriate help-wanted ads. If you have not been getting much response to your applications based on these ads, take another hard look at your resume and cover letter. Are you still customizing them for the jobs you really want? Or have you grown a little tired and started to send out cookie-cutter documents that look like everyone else's? Think creative. Think TQM.
- **Research.** Visit the library. Saturday is a good day to browse. Ask the librarians if they have any current newsletters published by local companies. Check the *Value Line Investment Survey,* which analyzes about 50 companies in depth each quarter. Browse through several sections, looking for companies in your specialty. Are some on your job prospect list? Make notes. Are they competitors of companies on your list? Make notes. Also look at recent quarterly editions of *Moody's Investor Services* for similar information.
- Complete your five Job Prospect Cards.
- **Network!** Saturdays are often good days to call additional social contacts for help and information. Are you running dry of names? What about those people you met on vacation last winter? Check your desk for any membership lists of golf clubs, tennis clubs, or aerobic classes.
- If your budget will allow, take your spouse, family, or a friend out for pizza or Chinese tonight. Share with them the good or the disappointing things that have happened to you during your job search. Thank them for any help they've given you.

What Other Types of Job Applicants Are You Competing Against?

Sun Tsu wrote, "If you know the enemy and know yourself, you need not fear the result of a hundred battles. If you know yourself but not the enemy, for every victory gained you will also suffer a defeat. If you know neither the enemy nor yourself, you will succumb in every battle."

DAY TWENTY-EIGHT SUNDAY

- **20-Minute Wake-up Exercise.** Why not ask a friend in business to walk along with you. You can discuss: When a company is ready to hire me, how will I handle salary negotiations, especially when the organization asks me to name a figure? I don't want to over- or underprice myself. *Suggestion:* Don't name an amount. Say you are eager to work for the company and ask them to say what they feel a superior performance in that position would merit. Ask for your friend's ideas.
- Complete five Job Prospect Cards, based on your past research. Then—
- Take the entire day off. Listen to music. Play golf. Enjoy some quiet time by yourself or with loved ones.

- **20-Minute Wake-up Exercise.** You're coming into the home stretch in your 30-day program. Ask yourself: Should I work even faster and more efficiently to reach hiring authorities and in "asking for the order"?
- **Media Review.** Review and reread the newspapers, trade magazines, and newsletters. Clip and save relevant information about your industries of choice and about each of your job prospect organizations. Answer any appropriate help-wanted ads. While you probably could answer these ads in your sleep, try to make each response fresh. One of the biggest problems of amateur actors in a long run of a play is that they become bored with their lines. And so, of course, does the audience. Look at every application as a "first night" and prepare it with all the enthusiasm and creativity you put into the first ones you sent out.
- **Research.** Complete at least five Job Prospect Cards. Keep "thinking small" in some of your selections. Remember, small companies are generating most of the jobs today.
- Send a letter to the CEOs of each of the five companies.
- Reread your Contact Notebook with a red marker in hand, starting from the first day you began making notes. Put a red mark by every single person you contacted by mail or phone who has not gotten back to you.
- **Network!** Spend the rest of the day trying to reach as many of these individuals by phone as you can. Your goals remain the same: To gain more information about the company, more referrals to other individuals within the company, and a chance to come in for a face-to-face talk.

"Tell me a story."

Want to prolong a conversation so you can gather more information or gain more time to make a good impression? Use one of the oldest attention-getting devices: Tell a story. Briefly describe one of your career successes in a problem/solution story. "We were monitoring a pipeline in Texas when we detected a sudden dangerous loss of pressure . . ." (then tell what you or your team did). Stories, metaphors, and analogies will bring your interviews and letters to life.

DAY THIRTY TUESDAY—GRADUATION DAY

- **20-Minute Wake-up Exercise.** Skip your exercise this morning and take an extra-long time over breakfast. Ask yourself: What have I learned about myself during this program? Are there areas in my background and education that I could enhance for continued career advancement? How have prospective employers been responding to me? Are there areas where I need to fine-tune my approaches to my colleagues and my work?
- **Media Review.** Review the local papers. Check any advertising columns in the business section. When companies announce a major new advertising campaign, they may be expanding their production line or sales force. Add them to your Job Prospect Cards. Clip and save all relevant articles. Respond to all appropriate help-wanted ads.
- **Research.** Complete at least five Job Prospect Cards.
- Review the help-wanted ads you responded to last week. Send a second letter and resume to those ads of particular interest to you.
- **Network!** Continue the comprehensive follow-up you started yesterday. Call any people you have been unable to reach at your five targeted companies. Make this your day for tying up all loose ends in your job search.
- **Celebrate!** Plan a celebratory dinner with someone you care about, either at home or on the town.

You have now completed your 30-day job-hunting program, and we hope that you are celebrating a new job tonight. But even if you're still looking, congratulations are still in order. By sticking with this program for 30 days, you have demonstrated both stamina and determination—two qualities that will help you find employment much faster than your competitors.

Also, in following this program you have compiled a complete self-inventory of your skills and background in your Life Experience Cards. You have contacted dozens of hiring authorities, stirring embers that could result in calls, interviews, and employment in the immediate future. And by now you have completed at least 150 Job Prospect Cards and conducted extensive research in your chosen industry and on five targeted companies, providing you with priceless employment contacts for immediate use and for use in advancing your career in the future.

As CEO, marketing director, and treasurer of You, Inc., this past month you have developed some new business skills that will help you in temp or contract work or even in starting your own business.

You have proven that you are not a passive victim of the whims of the economy. You have learned how to take charge of your life and your search for employment.

Some human resource experts are now predicting that the average individual may have up to 20 jobs in his or her lifetime. Today you are much better equipped to compete in this constantly changing employment world. You have learned a great new skill.

You know how to get a job!

NEXT STEPS

If You Have Found a Job

Within the next week send thank-you notes to everyone who helped you. You may also want to send a small gift to each member of your "Board of Advisers."

Keep the names, addresses, and phone numbers of everyone you contacted on file. Continue to add to this list in the months ahead. The network you've created can be of invaluable help as you continue to build your career.

Continue to complete your Life Experience Cards as you learn new skills in your new position. These cards can help you customize a resume in minutes when you see another position that interests you.

Give this program to a friend who's looking for work.

If You Are Still Looking

Take a long weekend to rest. Then start into another 30-day program next Monday. Don't lose the momentum you've built up!

- **Follow-up.** Contact each of the hiring authorities on your list. Jobs that were not available last month could be opening up next week. It's a moving parade.
- Pay close attention to those five companies you've targeted as your best prospects. In the case of smaller companies where you feel you've already talked with everyone in a position to hire you, you may want to change targets and choose another organization. In case of larger companies with dozens of hiring authorities, keep those phones ringing. You have already invested a great deal of time in learning about those companies. Keep gathering more information and more names of people within the company you can talk with.
- If funds are growing short, consider your other alternatives— including temp or contract work. (These are the fastest growing fields in the job market.) Both of these alternatives can lead to

permanent employment. If not, you've bought more time to pursue the career you really want.

Good luck!

> *Blessed is he who has found his work;*
> *let him ask no other blessedness.*

—Thomas Carlyle

Part IV

64 Strategic Projects to Help You Get a Job in 30 Days

Nothing is more dangerous than an idea . . . when you have only one.

—Philosopher Emile Chartier

T hroughout this program we've stressed using tried-and-true job-getting techniques as well as new ideas to give yourself a creative edge over other job applicants. We've also stressed the importance of following a daily structure to reach as many hiring authorities as possible.

We also want to arm you with a whole arsenal of additional ideas to keep your job search working on many different fronts. Many of these are adaptations of techniques used in advertising, marketing, and journalism to gain favorable attention. Some emphasize ideas suggested earlier in this book. Other techniques come from successful job hunters. Still others we used in finding jobs for ourselves.

Start by reading through this entire list. Check those that you feel would be most useful in your job search. These projects can also trigger your imagination as you think of other ways to capture the eyes and minds of hiring authorities.

During each day of this 30-day program we ask you to try several of these Strategic Projects. If one or more are especially productive for you in getting a response from prospective employers, keep repeating them.

Here are the ideas that can help accelerate your job search.

1. Spend two hours listing *all* the organizations you have ever belonged to and all the names you can recall of people you've met at those clubs, churches, and social groups—or people you've met at school, previous jobs, training seminars, conferences, conventions, etc. You may be amazed at how many people you've actually met over the last several years. Check through your desk drawers for business cards you've collected. These people can become part of your personal network. Tell them about your job search and send them your resume. *Never* be shy about letting people know you are looking for a job; that's not unusual in today's economy! Ask their opinions about local companies, a discussion that could lead to more names of hiring authorities for your Job Prospect Cards.

2. Form a job-hunting club. Call three people who are looking for work and have different job skills than you (so you won't be competing for the same jobs). For example, if you are a commercial artist, you could invite a teacher, engineer, and welder to join your club. Each is committed to coming up with *at least two job leads* every week for every other member of the group. When the engineer goes for a plant interview, she can also check that company's personnel bulletin board for job openings for teachers, welders, and commercial artists! *Advantage:* Everyone in the club gets at least six new job leads each week.

3. Offer friends and relatives a 15 percent reward for a lead that turns into a job. That's 15 percent of your first month's salary—strong motivation for others to be your eyes and ears in the job market. And it costs you nothing if you don't get a job. Yes, friends and relatives are already supposed to be looking for leads for you, but a cash reward seems to help people focus.

4. Draw a circle with a 50-mile radius around your home. Check in your local Yellow Pages for the names of newspapers within this circle. You may be surprised to find some you've never heard of. Write to the publications for sample copies. Subscribe to those that have extensive help-wanted listings.

5. Check the Interstate Job Bank at state or federal employment offices. This bank lists about 6,000 jobs available all over the country, often on microfiche. The employment office will show you how to use the microfiche viewer.

6. When you respond to a "help wanted" ad, ask a third party to write a cover letter for your resume on his or her letterhead. A letter that describes your skills and achievements will be much more credible coming from a third party than from you. The higher-up the executive ladder that individual is, the more effective this kind endorsement letter can be. You can help draft the letter during a phone conversation.

7. Interested in working for a nonprofit organization? Write to ACCESS for information about their monthly publication *Community Jobs*. A three-month subscription costs $29. *Advantage*: These jobs are not widely advertised (because nonprofits don't have the money), so you will probably face less competition. For more information, contact ACCESS, 50 Beacon Street, Boston, MA 02108; 617-720-5627.

8. Call or visit the placement office of your old school(s). Many schools today continue to serve alumni even many years after they've graduated. Talk with a counselor for job leads and referrals. These offices are often excellent sources of trade directories, computerized job bank programs, and career books. Also try other schools in your area. Even if you didn't go to school there, many of these offices let you use their facilities when they know you're looking for work or if you mention the name of a professor or school official who referred you to them.

9. Did you belong to a fraternity or sorority? Write to the headquarters to request back issues of alumni newsletters. Send the same request to the alumni office of your old school(s). These publications frequently carry class notes that list names, promotions, recent alumni achievements. Mark those in your field and add them to your networking list ("A" priority!).

10. Volunteer for a charitable or cultural organization in your community. Look through the organization's literature for names of volunteers who are executives from companies you would like to work for. You will often have a good chance to meet and network with them. When you volunteer, you also acquire more skills that you can list on your resume. Just don't volunteer too much time during your intensive job search. Keep your mind set on *getting a job!*

11. Let your fingers do a random walk through the phone book. Pick up the Yellow Pages. Turn to page five, fifth company from the top. Review your Life Experience Cards and look for a match with this organization. Do you have any special skills you could offer an electrical supply firm? No match? Try page ten, sixth company from the bottom. What could you offer this company? If you find your past experience could help that company, call or write to the organization immediately. This "random thinking" helps you break out of the rut and makes you realize you have many different skills that you could offer to many different companies. For more information about how to use random thinking in your life, read Edward de Bono's superb book *I Am Right, You Are Wrong.*

12. Call up two or three former co-workers in the evening. Ask them to candidly describe what they consider to be your major strengths and weaknesses. Ask them to recall what projects you handled well in your previous job. Ask them for names of other people you might contact for information about jobs. Make notes as you talk with them. This exercise may help you recall skills you can add to your Life Experience Cards. You also have new names for your "cold" calls tomorrow. (See—your network is growing!)

13. Call several temp agencies in your area. (Temp workers now include executives who work at high hourly fees in marketing and management.) Some will provide training in computer and secretarial skills. There's a good chance that a temp job will lead to a full-time position since you're meeting people and demonstrating your skills. Temp work is also not bad for a shrinking checking account. (We suggest using temp work as a contingency plan. If you do not have the job you want in 30 days, you may want to do some part-time temp work as you continue your job search.)

14. Call an insurance agent, and tell him or her that you are looking for a job and would appreciate any leads. These agents are often master networkers who can give you valuable contacts in many different industries. For example, we recently talked with an agent friend who has compiled names of executives of every major local company. Insurance agents are usually outgoing people who enjoy helping others. Of course, they also realize you will be an excellent prospect for their services once you've found employment.

15. If you belong to one of the airline clubs, visit the club once or twice in the next week. These clubs are perfect places to strike up conversations with traveling businesspeople who often are senior executives. Exchange business cards. If a company looks promising, write to your contact the next day to inquire about applying for a position. Never be afraid to ask for job-getting advice. Almost everybody loves to give advice. Don't you?

16. Looking for a job with an association? The American Society of Association Executives operates an executive search and referral service. The cost for nine months is $40 for members, $80 for nonmembers. Call 202-626-2750 for more information.

17. Read the *Wall Street Journal* Tuesday editions (which have the heaviest concentration of help-wanted ads). Subscribe or read it for free at your public library.

18. Need names for today's Job Prospect Cards? Ask the library for a copy of *Job Hunters Sourcebook: Where to Find Employment Leads and Other Job Search Resources* (Gale Research, Inc.).

19. Advertise your qualifications in the Peterson's Connexion, a computer-based job referral system used by Pepsi-Cola, Xerox, and other top companies. Annual cost for a listing is $40. (Free listings are available for undergraduate college students and recent grads.) For more information, call 800-338-3282.

20. Are you a closet Tom Brokaw or Dan Rather? Even if you don't have golden tonsils, there are many positions in broadcasting, ranging from sales to writing and production. The National Association of Broadcasters Employment Clearinghouse matches job hunters' qualifications with current job openings. No fee. Call 202-429-5498 for more information.

21. Are you currently in the Army? Check the *Army Employer Network Data Base,* a computer program that lists thousands of companies looking for people with military backgrounds. This data base is available now at 52 Army bases. You can also access a computer service that can help you convert your military experience into civilian job categories. (Many resumes from veterans confuse civilian personnel departments who are unclear about military titles and jargon.) Veterans get preference for federal jobs, and—here's a little-known fact—*spouses* of soldiers leaving the Army can also use this computer job service free of charge.

22. Check the *National Business Employment Weekly,* which combines a week's worth of help-wanted advertisements from all regional editions of the *Wall Street Journal.* To find the nearest distributor, call 800-JOB-HUNT.

23. Join one of the local job-hunting clubs or organizations listed by region in the Calendar of Events in the *National Business Employment Weekly.* These clubs are excellent places to network and exchange job leads.

24. Go to your public library and check help-wanted ads that are at least six months old. This gives you a list of companies that have been hiring in your field—companies you might not know about because they are not currently running ads. Contact them with an application and resume. Why? Six months is a typical trial period for many companies. Your resume could arrive when people they hired six months ago are leaving.

25. Send out a "broadcast" letter and resume to the personnel departments of every single company listed on your Job Prospect Cards. While we still recommend contacting individual hiring authorities within these companies (via separate and customized resumes directed at their particular needs), there's always the possibility that your letter could arrive just as personnel is to begin a search for a new opening. Job hunting is roulette. Cover as many numbers as you can!

26. Are you over 50? Call the Senior Career Planning and Placement Services, at 212-529-6660. This organization could help find you a volunteer position with a charitable organization or a paying job with an organization in your area.

27. Want to put some international business experience on your resume? Many American companies are looking for people who can function and succeed in the new global marketplace. You could work as a volunteer in the former Soviet Union or Eastern Europe. For example, some U.S. manufacturing executives have spent time in Poland helping a factory become more productive; still others have advised fledgling capitalists in Russia on how to use marketing more effectively. Benefits include free air transportation and free housing. For more information, contact the Citizens Democracy Corps Business Entrepreneur Program, at 800-394-1945.

28. Check in local newspapers for job fairs coming to your area. Check which companies are participating, then send them your application/resume before the fair. Often these fairs are annual events held by colleges or community organizations. You can anticipate one coming up by checking last year's papers.

29. If you are a military officer (active or retired or a warrant officer of the Army, Navy, Air Force, Marine Corps, Coast Guard, or Public Health Service), call the Retired Officers Association for valuable job-hunting help; 800-245-TROA. Ask for a free copy of *Marketing Yourself for a Second Career* (it's excellent). Ask about becoming a member in the organization ($20 annually); membership allows you to register in their computerized job-referral service.

30. Look for out-of-the-ordinary ways to attract the attention of employers. For example, write a letter to the editor of the local paper in which you demonstrate your expertise or analytical ability. Volunteer to appear on a discussion panel at the PTA or your professional society. Become your own press agent (yes, you are also Public Relations Director of You, Inc.).

31. Go to a speech given by an influential executive. If there is a question-and-answer period afterward, ask a question about something that was mentioned in the speech. Then write to that executive on the next day, complimenting him or her and expressing your interest in this subject. Ask if you can visit the executive briefly to discuss it further. During this discussion you can also begin asking questions about the executive's company. Tell the person you are looking for a position in the same industry, and ask for names of individuals who can provide you with more information. Then call them. Also remember to network with other members of the audience before and after the speech. People attracted to these types of speeches are often themselves hiring authorities.

32. Visit trade shows in your field, which are an excellent way to network with executives who could hire you. Pass out business cards, and don't be shy about asking for job leads. Often you can get into trade shows just by showing a business card, which is another good reason to print your own.

33. Want a government job? The U.S. government now has its own job hotline. It costs a modest 40 cents a minute. A recorded voice will ask you various questions about your work experience, education, and geographic preferences. You answer by touching numbers on a touch-tone phone. The recording then tells you which federal jobs are available to suit your qualifications and preferences. Call 900-990-9200.

Other good sources of government job listings are the *Federal Jobs Digest* (six bi-weekly issues, $29; for more information, call 800-824-5000) and *The Federal Research Service* (a newsletter about government job openings and an electronic job-search service; for more information, call 703-281-0200).

Don't forget that the federal government fills 2,000 to 4,200 job vacancies every week!

34. Would your career benefit by working overseas with the U.S. Peace Corps? You can get valuable international experience—with all living expenses paid, plus a $4,800 cash bonus and a free college scholarship when you return home. This offer is not just for recent grads. Many people suffering from mid-career job burnout have found a new life in the Peace Corps. For more information, call 800-424-8580.

35. Call the personnel departments of major companies and ask if they have a job hotline. Many do. Also check company listings in the telephone White Pages for any "Job Opportunity" numbers. Call these hotlines regularly to check on current availabilities. Then respond immediately.

36. Reread all of the resumes and cover letters you have sent out to date. A few days away from these materials will give you a fresh perspective. You may find awkward phrases or misspellings that you might have missed but can correct in future mailings.

37. Place a small ad about yourself in your local newspaper—on the business or sports pages, but *not* in the classified section. Stress in the headline what added value you can bring to the fortunate company that hires you. For example:

Seasoned computer expert can help you reduce your information storage costs by 50%.

Photocopy the ad and send it to key executives of your target companies. Attach a short note, such as, "Did you see this in this morning's newspaper?" In this media-hype world, being in the paper makes you a "celebrity for a day." Make the most of it.

38. Read trade magazines in your field. Make notes of personnel changes. This gives you valuable clues as to which compa-nies are hiring and firing. Write to newly promoted executives with a note of congratulation. Tell them you are interested in serving on their new team. Many newly hired or promoted exec-utives often hire a brand-new team, especially if they have been brought in because sales are sagging or production is falling. If they think you are someone who could help them solve the prob-lems they've inherited, you could get a call sooner than you ex-pect.

Reading trade papers regularly also helps to keep you up to speed on buzzwords in the industry. You could use some of these phrases in your cover letters and interviews to show you're "in the loop." For example, current buzzwords in many businesses now include "empowerment," "TQM—Total Quality Management," etc. Build your own business vocabulary.

39. Have a favorite professor or teacher at school? Call him or her today. At the end of the conversation, ask for job leads.

40. Collect current catalogs of colleges and high schools offering special programs or adult education programs. Many of these courses and seminars are taught by local business execu-tives. Call such an executive and ask for more information on the course. This kind of query often gets you past the gatekeepers because many execs want to "sell" their course to as many people as possible. This networking contact could lead to a further meet-ing and a discussion of employment opportunities.

41. Enroll in one of these part-time courses (in the evening, of course, when it won't interfere with your full-time job of get-ting a job). These classes are excellent places for more network contacts. Do the best you possibly can and speak up in class. Then hit the executive for a job interview (or job leads) at the end of the course. Some will feel a moral obligation to help their stu-dents.

42. Call several friends and ask for the names of people at their companies who have recently been hired. Then call these people (using your friends' names as referrals) and ask them for the secrets of their success. Most newly hireds are in a state of euphoria and happy to talk about their achievements. You may pick up some additional job-hunting tips, but most importantly, you are building your network. Ask also for the names of the individuals who interviewed the recently hired person. Add this information to your Job Prospect Card on that company.

43. Join one or more organizations where you could meet people in a position to hire you—such as the Lions or Kiwanis or the various men's and women's professional organizations. If you're not ready to join full-time, find a member among your network and see if you can go as a guest.

44. Volunteer as a speaker for a local service club (they are almost always looking for speakers). Address an issue that demonstrates your expertise or experience in solving problems. Example: "How micromarketing could bring new industry to our community." Write this speech and send a copy with a short note to the CEOs of all your target companies. Then call them for a discussion about their company. They may have heard about you. Send a copy of your speech to the local newspaper. Self-publicity is a valuable job-hunting tool.

45. Subscribe to the bimonthly *Search Bulletin,* a good listing of *unadvertised* executive positions that features 80 to more than 100 new jobs per issue. It's also available by MCI Mail in your computer. Call 800-486-9220 for more information.

46. Check newspaper calendars of events for business breakfasts, seminars, community meetings, etc. Attend some of these events and talk with people you meet. Collect and exchange business cards. These meetings are excellent sources of names for your network. To be sure you're prepared, write a 30-second "script" about yourself that you can use at various network meetings, breakfasts, etc. Example: "I'm very pleased to meet you. My name is Mary Erwin. I am a legal secretary formerly with Bowen & Bowen. I am now looking for similar work."

You never know when this kind of introduction could lead into a longer conversation and specific job leads. And don't worry about being "pushy." The people you meet are usually there to sell you something, too!

47. Based on the research you've completed to date, write an outline describing what you feel are the common major problems among the companies you've targeted—falling sales, stagnant growth, labor problems, etc. What could you do to help solve these problems? This is an excellent angle from which to approach your job interviews with these companies, since most companies aren't really interested in you as a person, as charming and pleasant as you may be. They want to know *what you can do for them.*

48. Call at least five or six people (former teachers, supervisors, bosses, clergy) to ask if you could use them as references. When they agree, send each of them a thank-you note and a copy of your resume. Your note should also tell them what your job objective is. This information can help them give more targeted answers when prospective employers call about you. *References today are usually checked.*

49. Call the Economic Development Agency in your hometown (almost every community has an agency with this or a similar name). This organization is charged with the job of attracting more businesses to your area. Find out which companies are coming and contact these organizations by phone to check their future employment needs. You want to reach them *before* they place help-wanted ads.

50. Call one or more account executives at local brokerage firms. Ask about "hot" local companies—those that are increasing sales, expanding, or opening a new office or store. Many brokerage firms also publish newsletters with the same information. Contact these expanding businesses immediately and get your application in their hands.

51. Check building permits in your local newspaper, which is a good way to learn which new companies are coming to town and which local businesses may be expanding. Each one of these companies is now a potential employer. Real estate agents, lawyers, and contractors can also provide this kind of information.

52. Spend an hour on the phone this evening with old friends, schoolmates, etc., to discuss your job search. While they may not know of any job openings, ask them if they personally know of anyone who could help you or provide you with information about a particular industry. Then ask if you can use your friends' names when you contact these people. "Knowing somebody who knows somebody" is still often the best way to get a job or an informational interview.

53. Call the personnel departments of several major companies. Ask which employment agencies and specific job counselors they work with. Then call those counselors. Give the name of the human resources/personnel director who referred you. That person is the employment agency's client. That means your application will probably get a lot more personal attention.

54. Visit your local chamber of commerce. Most have free directories that list member companies. These directories also list the company executive who represents that organization in the chamber. Many of them are important hiring authorities within their companies. Go as a guest to some of the meetings. If the annual membership fee is modest, you might consider joining. Call the chamber's executive director and schedule a meeting. Their job is to meet people, and they are usually very knowledgeable about which businesses are expanding. Ask for the names of people you might call. The name of the chamber's director often opens executive doors.

55. Go on a bulletin board hunt. Visit several federal, state, and large corporate office buildings and look for hallway bulletin boards. Often new jobs are posted on these boards. To get into the inner hallways of some larger corporations, tell the receptionist you want to visit the personnel department to pick up an application (where most of the openings are posted anyway) or a customer service department to pick up sales literature about their products or services. Then "shop" bulletin boards along the way.

56. Call the editor of a local newspaper or magazine and volunteer to write an article about a particular company. You probably won't get an assignment from the *Washington Post* or the *New York Times*, but there are thousands of tiny publications that would welcome contributions—especially because you aren't asking for money. This assignment is your "open sesame" to dozens of executives in that industry. Few executives can resist an ego-flattering opportunity to be interviewed. You will learn more about the industry and add many new contact names to your network list. Always send a copy of the published article to everyone you interviewed, which is yet another opportunity for contact and follow-up discussions that could lead to a job.

57. Spend a few minutes each Sunday looking at large display ads for positions outside your field in the help-wanted section of the newspaper. These ads reveal which companies are growing and may also need people of your specialty.

58. When you find your job, help someone else who's looking. Share this book with them. It's a tough world out there when you're searching for employment. He or she jests who never felt the emotional wound of a pink slip. There's even a bonus for doing good. Every job seeker you help becomes part of your growing Lifetime Network—the new necessity of career building in the '90s!

59. Check the situations-wanted ads in newspapers and trade magazines placed by people looking for the same type of job you are. Write to them and offer to swap your rejects (companies that have turned you down) for their rejects. They have nothing to lose and neither do you. But what you have to gain are new prospects for which you might be a better fit than the original applicant—and vice versa. The person you wrote to is also one more person you can add to your growing network.

60. Offer a "premium" to increase response to your direct-mail campaign. You've been gathering a great deal of information about your targeted companies and about the industry you are now in (or want to enter). This could include news clips, comments you've heard from the companies' employees, information you've gathered from their present clients, etc. Condense this information into a short two- to three-page report that you offer to send to the company president or hiring authority. For example, at the end of your initial letter of application you could add this P.S.: "I have been studying your company and industry closely in recent weeks. I have just completed a short report for my own use in interviews, but perhaps you would be interested in seeing some of the interesting things I have heard from some of your clients. I would be happy to send you a copy."

You're ahead of the game in two ways. You can send a report that demonstrates your ability to analyze and communicate clearly. And it would be a stone-hearted (and probably unsuccessful) CEO who would not want to see what clients say about his or her company!

61. Call AT&T at 800-426-8686 and order a toll-free 800-number business-to-business directory. This book lists over 120,000 companies nationwide, categorized by industry, and is invaluable when you are doing research on a specific industry and want to talk with various hiring authorities but don't want to run up big long-distance bills. The cost of the directory is $14.95. Why not ask a willing spouse or friend to call 50 or 100 companies in a day, ask for the personnel department, and inquire about any current availabilities. If they come up with a live one, you then follow up immediately.

62. Think "small"! That's where the action in hiring is today. Call your local chamber of commerce for the names and companies of individuals who have been named "small business-people of the year." Most of these people are accessible. Call them up to congratulate them. Chances are their companies are expanding and they may need someone like you.

63. If you bank with a large institution or do business with a large law firm, ask them about any referral service they offer. Many of the larger companies will refer executives to their clients who may be looking for new people. It's a form of networking that helps these companies serve clients and build loyalty among those freshly hired.

64. When you read your local newspaper's business section, look for stories about companies with problems. Forget your occupational specialty for a moment. Do you have any skills or experience that could help that organization? If so, write to the president and explain what you can do. A CEO ultimately doesn't care what occupational label you put on yourself if you can solve one or more of the company's major problems. He or she could even create a new job for such a problem solver. It happens every day.

Hal Gieseking has enjoyed three careers—in advertising, in journalism, and now in helping people find jobs. He is president of The Career Advisor, Inc., and his job-getting tips have been featured on the front page of *USA Today,* in the Associated Press, in numerous newspapers and magazines, and on more than 100 radio and TV stations. He develops career workshops for the Special Programs division of the College of William and Mary. In his earlier careers in New York City, he was a creative supervisor for the advertising agency Ogilvy & Mather, Inc., and later president of his own advertising and marketing company. In his third career, as a journalist, he has served as consumer editor of the Reader's Digest's *Travel/Holiday* magazine, written more than 300 national magazine articles and 10 books, and appeared on "CBS Morning News" as travel correspondent.

During 20 years with *Kiplinger's Personal Finance* magazine (formerly *Changing Times*), Paul Plawin covered the jobs and careers beat. He conducted surveys of corporate recruiters to compile Kiplinger's annual report on jobs for new college graduates. He has interviewed hundreds of career counselors, psychologists, executive search consultants, personnel directors, hiring managers, and management gurus—as well as people looking for jobs. He has also worked as a writer and editor for national publications that include *Southern Living* and *Better Homes and Gardens,* and he edited careers newspaper supplements for Sun Features, Inc. He is currently an executive with the American Vocational Association, which represents America's vocational-technical education community.

Win a Canadian Rockies Vacation for Two

NORTHWEST
A I R L I N E S

- **Round-trip air transportation via Northwest Airlines (U.S. Gateway Cities) to Vancouver, British Columbia**
- **3 nights at the Waterfront Centre Hotel, a "downtown jewel" in Vancouver with a mountain and harbor view**
- **A spectacular train trip on the "Rocky Mountaineer"—a 2-day ride past snow-capped peaks, lakes, and ancient forests**
- **2 nights deluxe accommodations at the new Rimrock Resort Hotel, with an awesome view of Banff and Bow Valley**

Tell us how this book helped you find a job in 30 days or less—briefly describe your successful job search in less than 150 words. For example, you might tell which job-getting techniques attracted the attention of your new employer or how you gave yourself a "creative edge" to separate yourself from your competition. Send your essay on or before December 31, 1994 to Canadian Rockies Contest, Simon & Schuster, 1230 Avenue of the Americas, New York, NY 10020, Attn: S. H. Fleming.

The authors of *30 Days to a Good Job* will select the winning essay based primarily on the originality and creativity used in applying the techniques of this book in finding a new job. Good luck in your job search . . . and next year you just might be celebrating your new position on a vacation in one of the most beautiful high spots of North America—the Canadian Rockies. See page 220 for Official Rules.

30 Days to a Good Job
Official Contest Rules

Win a One-Week Vacation for Two
in the Canadian Rockies
(Void in VT, FL, MD, AZ, and the Province of Quebec)

1. Contest Prize: A trip for two for six nights and seven days to the Canadian Rockies, including double-occupancy hotel room and round-trip airfare to Vancouver from Northwest Airlines' Gateway Cities in the U.S. with return from Calgary to Northwest Airlines' Gateway Cities in the U.S. (All transportation arrangements and expenses to and from Northwest Airlines' Gateway Cities in the U.S. are the winner's responsibility.) Trip includes three nights in Vancouver at the Waterfront Centre Hotel (right on the waterfront); two days daylight ride through the Canadian Rockies on the "Rocky Mountaineer" (past glaciers, waterfalls, and wildlife, with an overnight stay at Kamloops); and two nights at the Rimrock Resort Hotel (built right on the edge of a breathtaking view of the Rockies and the beautiful resort town of Banff). (Approximate retail value is U.S. $3,500. Actual retail value of prize will depend on points of departure and return.) Trip subject to availability, certain blackout dates apply, and must be taken no later than December 31, 1995.

2. Print or type an original essay, no more than 150 words, describing "how you found a job within 30 days using *30 Days to a Good Job.*" Include your name, address, zip code, and day/evening phone numbers. Your entry must be original and must neither have been submitted to nor published by any other publication. Open to Canadian and U.S. residents, aged 18 or older. Sponsors' employees (and their immediate families), their respective subsidiaries, affiliates, and advertising and promotion agencies are not eligible. Taxes are the responsibility of the winner. Void in VT, FL, MD, and AZ, and the Province of Quebec, and wherever else prohibited by law. Prize will be awarded. No substitution, transfer, or cash redemption of prizes permitted. *U.S. Residents Only:* Proof of purchase is required (original cash register receipt with price circled). Canadian residents can read and review the book at their local libraries.

3. Selection of winners: Hal Gieseking and Paul Plawin, authors of *30 Days to a Good Job,* will review and judge all essays on the basis of originality, 30 percent; creativity, 30 percent; enthusiasm, 20 percent; and presentation, 20 percent. All decisions of the judges are final.

4. Mail completed essay, and for U.S. residents proof of purchase, first class, to: Canadian Rockies Contest, Simon & Schuster, 1230 Avenue of the Americas, New York, New York 10020. Attn: S. H. Fleming. All entries must be received by December 31, 1994 and none will be returned. One entry per person, family, or household.

5. Potential winner will be notified by mail on or about February 1, 1995 and will be asked to sign an Affidavit of Eligibility and Release. The Affidavit must be returned within 14 days of notification or an alternate winner may be selected.

6. All entries become the property of Simon & Schuster, Inc. and Hal Gieseking and Paul Plawin, as Sponsors, and may be used for purposes of promotion, advertising, and for merchandising, except where prohibited by law. Sponsors will not be responsible for lost, late, or misdirected mail. Winner grants to Sponsors the right to use his/her name, likeness, and essay for any advertising, promotional, or trade purpose, without further compensation to or permission from winner.

7. Winner and his/her travel companion release Sponsors from any claim or action, including but not limited to, personal injury or property damage, arising out of acceptance of the contest prize.

8. For winner's list, send a #10 self-addressed stamped envelope between February 15, 1995 and May 30, 1995 to: Canadian Rockies Contest, Simon & Schuster, 1230 Avenue of the Americas, New York, New York 10020, Attn.: S. H. Fleming.